It's easy to get caught up in the [...] primary call to be disciple-mak[...] and profound reminder that the effectiveness of the gospel in our time hinges on our capacity to disciple the nations.

ALAN HIRSCH
Award-winning author on missional Christianity and founder of Forge Mission Training Network

Central to movement is the grassroots work of making disciples. In *Guardrails*, Alan Briggs calls believers to move from being couch potatoes who accumulate information to being movement makers who intentionally focus on multiplying Kingdom-oriented apprentices of Jesus in the local church. The strength of the book is that he gives us a sticky and SHARRP (Simple, Holistic, Adaptable, Regular, Reproducible, and Positive) way to do this. The most beautiful thing about this book is that Alan embodies the message he shares.

J. R. WOODWARD
National Director of V3 Church Planting Movement and coauthor of *The Church as Movement*

Maybe you, like me, can feel stuck and tired at times (on the ministry treadmill, as Alan calls it), and yet there is a longing, a desire, to be part of a *movement*, a movement of the Kingdom of God. I was hungry and eager for a book like this. I needed to read this book, as it met me in all those places of longing and called me into more.

KATIE FOWLER
Associate pastor for Missional Strategies, First Presbyterian Church, Colorado Springs

Missionaries and church planters do not simply appear. They are discovered, developed, and deployed. Within the pages of *Guardrails* you will uncover not only the foundations for a multiplying church but also the practical application of being a church who raises up and sends out a generation of gospel-centered world changers. Alan Briggs is a leader with a proven track record of making disciples who make disciples. This book is dangerous because it will change the fabric of church, but it's a journey worth taking.

DUSTIN WILLIS
Director of the SEND Network, author of *Life in Community*, and coauthor of *Life on Mission*

I'm a big fan of Alan Briggs. He is not only a thinker. He is also a practitioner and coach. And when you put those realities together, you have something special. Add in Alan's infectious passion and intense creativity, and you get something magical. That's exactly what *Guardrails* is. Magical. This is a much-needed book, coming at the right time to spark multiplication among God's people.

DANIEL FUSCO
Lead pastor of Crossroads Community Church, Vancouver, Washington, and author of *Honestly: Getting Real about Jesus and Our Messy Lives*

Clear. Concise. Thorough. Engaging. Practical. Powerful! Alan Briggs brings it all together in this book. The best part is that, with everything you'll read here, Alan has lived it out in real time with real people. He is relentless in his love for people outside the Kingdom of God and is equally invested in making and developing Kingdom disciples and leaders. Add to that his extensive interaction with some of the best thought-leaders and practitioners out there, and you have this amazing work that will absolutely, no doubt, help you take your next steps as a disciple, a disciple-maker, and a disciple leader. Yeah, it's that good!

KEVIN COLÓN
Pastor of Neighboring Way of Life at LifeBridge Christian Church, Longmont, Colorado

Alan Briggs isn't simply a writer sharing ideas; he's the real deal. In one of the most gospel-hostile environments in the country, Alan lives out the six multiplication principles he outlines in *Guardrails*. The structure he outlines is born out of years of one-on-one discipleship with leaders at every level. If you are serious about creating a multiplying discipleship culture in your church or ministry, I highly recommend this book.

GEOFF SURRATT
Pastor, leadership coach, and author of *Ten Stupid Things That Keep Churches from Growing*

Alan Briggs has produced a book that is eminently practical. You will read his heart in this book. Briggs cares deeply about seeing Christians understand the call to discipleship. The genius of this book is in its simplicity. Briggs intentionally outlines principles designed to be implemented. They're clear, straightforward, and ready for use. Embrace these principles and experience fresh discipleship.

CHRIS HORST
Director of Development at HOPE International and coauthor of *Mission Drift*

This is a great resource that will inspire, strengthen, and equip a wide variety of leaders. Alan writes with the eye of a practitioner who has also reflected well on what he does and why. Whether you're a planter or a leader in an established church, you will benefit from this book!

ALEX ABSALOM
Leader of Missional Innovation, Grace Church, Long Beach, California

Alan Briggs brings passion, creativity, and timeless Kingdom principles to the adventure of church planting. Over the past few years I've had the privilege of watching Alan live out the great commission lifestyle. In *Guardrails* he shares his adventure and the lessons he's learning. A great book! Don't miss it.

DAVID GARRISON
International missionary strategist and author of *Church Planting Movements* and *A Wind in the House of Islam*

Guardrails is a book for in-the-trenches leaders that is chock-full of great insights on the importance and practice of the discipleship process. Alan is the real thing, and this new book will be a great help to anyone seeking to use his or her one and only life for the King and his Kingdom.

TOM HUGHES
Co–lead Pastor, Christian Assembly Church, Los Angeles, California, and author of *Curious*

For those of us who are tired of rigid, simplistic, and lifeless formulas for discipleship, Alan's book is a refreshing well. He casts a vision of becoming apprentices of Jesus in a profound, accessible, and winsome manner. His six guardrails provide enough direction for healthy movement, yet enough freedom to embody apprenticeship in our own communal contexts.

DR. DREW MOSER
Dean of Experiential Learning, Taylor University

The secret to a multiplying church is multiplying people. For all the time that people have sat under faithful ministries, they've not been taught to be the multipliers that Jesus intended. How could we have gotten so far off course? Alan Briggs puts the guardrails up to keep ministry, church, and people back on the road to multiplication.

PEYTON JONES
West Region Director of Multiply Training, NAMB; founder of New Breed Church Planting; author of *Church Zero*

In its stripped-down and simplest form, church planting is about multiplication—multiplying disciples. As person after person responds to the gospel, each of them needs to be nurtured, challenged, and led into a deeper and more robust walk with Christ. Alan Briggs shows us practically how not only to disciple people but also to multiply disciples. He gives us the tools needed to move from addition to multiplication, which is essential for a church-planting movement.

SEAN BENESH
Author of *Exegeting the City* and *Blueprints for a Just City*

GUARDRAILS

six principles for a multiplying church

ALAN BRIGGS

A NavPress resource published in alliance
with Tyndale House Publishers, Inc.

NavPress is the publishing ministry of The Navigators, an international Christian organization and leader in personal spiritual development. NavPress is committed to helping people grow spiritually and enjoy lives of meaning and hope through personal and group resources that are biblically rooted, culturally relevant, and highly practical.

For more information, visit www.NavPress.com.

The Team:
Don Pape, Publisher
David Zimmerman, Acquisitions Editor
Mark Anthony Lane II, Designer

Library of Congress Cataloging-in-Publication Data

Names: Briggs, Alan, author.
Title: Guardrails : six principles for a multiplying church / Alan Briggs.
Description: Colorado Springs : NavPress, 2016. | Includes bibliographical references.
Identifiers: LCCN 2016015623 (print) | LCCN 2016025510 (ebook) |
    ISBN 9781631464355 | ISBN 9781631464386 (Apple) | ISBN 9781631464362
    (E-Pub) | ISBN 9781631464379 (Kindle)
Subjects: LCSH: Church growth. | Discipling (Christianity)
Classification: LCC BV652.25 .B754 2016 (print) | LCC BV652.25 (ebook) |
    DDC 253—dc23
LC record available at https://lccn.loc.gov/2016015623

Printed in the United States of America

22   21   20   19   18   17   16
 7   6   5   4   3   2   1

To Mom and Dad.

You embody Jesus. Thanks for accidentally training two pastors.

CONTENTS

FOREWORD

WHEN I FINISHED READING *Guardrails: Six Principles for a Multiplying Church*, my first reaction was to shake my head and say, "Wow, I wish I'd had this book when I was planting Community Christian Church!"

It was more than two decades ago that a group of friends from college sat in a breakfast restaurant dreaming about how God might use us by starting a new church. We had a vague vision of the church as a movement; we knew we wanted to plant churches, but there was so much we didn't know! And it took us a very, very long time to figure it out!

Community Christian Church eventually went on to have a dozen (and counting!) sites across Chicagoland and launch a network of hundreds of reproducing churches called NewThing. But we could have done so much more! It took us nine years before we ever started a new campus! And it took us twelve years before we ever planted a new church! I sometimes wonder what we were doing for the first decade.

And then I remember what we were doing: We were figuring out on our own how to be a multiplying church. As I said: "Wow, I wish I'd had this book when I was planting!"

What I needed then, and what most leaders need, is the kind of theologically grounded and practical ministry wisdom found in *Guardrails*. If we'd had the guidance and clear instruction that you are about to access through this book, we could have started thinking and behaving like a movement from the very beginning. Consequently, we would have planted more churches, apprenticed and released more leaders, and done so much more for the mission of Jesus!

Alan Briggs's *Guardrails* would have helped us. I believe it will help you in two very significant ways.

First, *Guardrails* offers *a simple understanding of movement thinking*. Before that first breakfast meeting to start Community Christian Church was over, we had scratched out the following three-phase vision for this new church:

- Phase 1: Impact Church
- Phase 2: Reproducing Church
- Phase 3: Movement

As we talked about being an impact church, we dreamed of a church that would grow to a certain size and would impact the neighborhood and community in such a powerful way that everyone in that community would see the positive impact we were making. When we described being a reproducing church, we thought about how one day we would plant churches both locally and globally. The third phase was a dream: If God would bless our efforts in phases one and two, we would eventually catalyze a movement of reproducing and impact-making churches. We had the vision and the holy ambition to be an Acts 1:8 church, but we did not understand how to do it!

In chapter 1 Briggs borrows Dee Hock's term *chaordic* to help us better understand that movement-making will always have enough *order* to give it a common purpose and direction, and enough *chaos* to give it permission and innovation. While movement-making was a part of our vision from the beginning, we didn't understand even the simplest ideas like this one. Chapter 11 of *Guardrails* is worth the price of the book as Alan holds our hands and explains how to apply movement-making principles. Read every word of this book and you will come to a clearer understanding of what movement is and how movement works.

Second, *Guardrails* offers *six simple principles for being a multiplying church*. Through my role as president of the Exponential Conference, I have the opportunity to influence thousands of church leaders and church planters. I take that responsibility very seriously, and we are currently challenging every church to become a "Level 5 Multiplying Church." The nomenclature of "Level 5 Multiplying Church" comes from the following labeling based on research of churches in North America:

- Level 1: Decline
- Level 2: Plateau (80 percent are in decline or plateaued)

- Level 3: Addition (16 percent are growing by addition)
- Level 4: Reproduce (4 percent have reproduced a new site or church)
- Level 5: Multiply (no churches currently are multiplying into movements)

Community Christian Church is still a Level 4 church with aspirations for becoming a Level 5. Alan Briggs offers us simple principles for becoming such a multiplying church. I wish we had had those six principles twenty years ago to build upon. I wish I had known then what Alan writes about in one of those six principles: that discipleship needs to be holistic. Maybe then I would not have burnt out so many artists, leaders, and volunteers. If you want to become a Level 5 multiplying church, put these six principles to work and do not waver.

I have only one critique of *Guardrails: Six Principles for a Multiplying Church*. Alan, you should have written this sooner. *Wow, I wish I'd had this book when I was planting Community Christian Church!*

Dave Ferguson
COMMUNITY—Lead Pastor
NewThing—Visionary Leader

INTRODUCTION

HOW WE STAYED AFLOAT

It was getting close to spring during my junior year of college. A few buddies and I decided to plan an epic spring-break adventure. To qualify as "epic," it needed to involve a challenge that we weren't sure we could actually pull off— a challenge that would blur the line between risky and just plain stupid.

After about half an hour of scheming and consulting a map, we decided we would spend several nights on a wilderness island in the Gulf of Mexico. We would get there by canoe.

Yep, that's right—canoe.

After a long drive from the Midwest, we opened the door to our van and smelled the salt water. We unloaded our canoes, packed our gear, revved ourselves up for the ordeal, and set off directly into the waves.

At first the waves weren't bad, but as we got out farther from shore, they got more choppy. In a few minutes they were pounding against our canoes, rocking us from side to side. We realized the island was farther away than we first imagined. The current was pushing us back, even as we paddled forward. Our little canoes began filling with water from the pounding waves, making every paddle stroke even more exhausting.

Suddenly things got urgent. And when that happened, something changed.

Our minds shifted from thinking about how hard the paddling was to working together as a team. We just needed to crest around the island, and then the waves would shift, pushing us onto the beach. We yelled instructions to each other. We played the roles that we played best. No fancy business—it was all-hands-on-deck and full-speed-ahead, with the laser focus of getting to the other side of the island.

Finally we dragged ourselves onto the beach, exhausted and drenched in sweat and seawater. For a few days we lived like Tom Hanks in the move *Cast Away.*

When I think about our epic adventure, I wonder: *How did we make it?* We weren't the strongest paddlers in the world, and none of us had ever canoed in the ocean. What made the difference for us?

- First of all, we were crazy enough to believe we could paddle the ocean.
- Second, the risk forced us to function as a team.
- Finally, we understood a few key principles of boating, and we applied them.

In many ways the great commission is like a canoe trip on the ocean. You have some equipment designed to help you make disciples. Your equipment may seem meager to you, but Jesus assures you it's enough to get the job done. We are not great, but we have most certainly been commissioned.

The equipment and the will are only part of the equation, however. Who will stay afloat in the epic quest to make disciples? It won't be the biggest churches or brightest leaders who effectively make disciples in the way of Jesus, but the ones who have identified a few key principles and committed to live by them. The great commission is an epic movement, but like any movement, its impact is enhanced or inhibited by decisions and commitments we make in advance.

The North American church is going through a wake-up call. God seems to be reawakening the collective heart of the church back to discipleship. Some of us have been jolted into action as our boats have been rocked. Others never stopped coasting and have woken up to find themselves adrift. In his grace, our Father uses many methods to wake his people up.

I talk with pastors, leaders, and "regular folks" everywhere who are no longer content simply listening to sermons and handing out bulletins. We're realizing healthy ministry always centers around making disciples. This is a huge and exciting realization for the church. It's a new move back to our original call.

We might recognize this call back to discipleship, but without properly defining *what* we are pursuing, we will continue to miss how to effectively pursue it. We have some unlearning and relearning to do. This is not something we can afford to miss.

In the midst of much frustration and limited capacity,

God gave me six movement principles—I call them *guardrails*—to keep me on track. For me and those I have discipled, the six guardrails outlined in this book have been a breath of fresh air. I have taught and reviewed them in small and midsized groups in coffee shops, greasy breakfast joints, classrooms, and living rooms. They aren't brilliant and radical. They are simple and usable. They have literally changed everything.

These principles brought me hope of fruitfulness in my own disciple-making ministry when I was overwhelmed. The leaders I've trained as apprentices, neighborhood missionaries, aspiring pastors, and church planters through Frontline Church Planting report that these six movement principles have structured their discipleship forever.

Educational training for ministry will always fall short. Even Jesus trained sparingly before releasing his band of followers onto a waiting world. No training process can teach every skill, every response, every piece of knowledge, or every biblical truth needed in church leadership. Our world changes too quickly for that.

But there is beauty found in guiding principles. They inform our simple obedience to Christ, empower us to trust the leadership of the Spirit, and give structure to our ever-adapting ministry. My prayer is that every read, every download, and every discussion on these guardrails for a multiplying church will advance the great commission from the ends of the earth to the heart of your parish. If you believe the church is the primary vehicle God will use to change the world, get ready. There's urgent work to be done.

PART ONE

FOUNDATIONS

CHAOS IN SEARCH OF ORDER

Style and structure are the essence of a book; great ideas are hogwash.
VLADIMIR NABOKOV

We cannot create movements; only the Spirit of God can. But we can align ourselves, raising the sails of kingdom-oriented ministry, so that when the Spirit does blow, we are ready to move forward.
STEVE SMITH

Discipleship and disciple-making is foundational to any movement. No matter which movement you observe you will find that they are obsessed with discipleship and disciple-making.
ALAN HIRSCH

IT WAS AN ORDINARY Tuesday afternoon. I was meeting with a church planter at a local coffee shop. For some reason, church planters and coffee go together like Portland and weird. After catching up a bit I asked a familiar question: "What is the next hump your church is facing?"

His response was simple. "If we just get over the one-hundred-person mark, we are going to be fine."

At the time their church was wrangling about forty folks into a Sunday worship gathering. He was wishing to more than double the size of his church. So my next question was, "If God brought you sixty people tomorrow, what would you do with them?"

It was obvious he had no idea.

I have had this exact thing happen at least three other times! Unfortunately, most churches have no idea what they would or should do with the people God brings them.

We often see people as solutions to our problems: Add sixty people and our church plant is out of the woods. God sees people differently—sixty people he created in his image; sixty people harassed and helpless, like sheep without a shepherd. God knows the plans he has for those sixty people; why would he trust us with them if we don't?

Just a few months later, this conversation would come back to haunt me. My heart cry is to influence leaders who are hungry to live like Jesus and multiply disciples. I meet with as many hungry leaders as I can. I create as many equipping venues as I have the influence to put together, which can lead people into a sustainable life of mission. Each day at 10:02 a.m., I pray as Jesus commanded in Luke 10:2: "The harvest is plentiful, but the laborers are few. Therefore pray earnestly to the Lord of the harvest to send out laborers into his harvest."

The problem with asking God for something is that once he gives us what we've asked for, it becomes our responsibility. The spirit is willing, but the flesh is weak and the calendar is already full. At a certain point I started feeling completely swamped, maxed out with no solutions on how to ease the load of administration and equipping leaders. My list was long, and the margin for error was minuscule. We had just adopted two kids from Ethiopia who didn't know our language, I was working an extra job on top of full-time ministry, and my wife was getting her master's degree in the evenings. We slept occasionally.

In the midst of this frantic season, God put two new men on my mind. I was convinced I didn't have time to insert these two new guys into my life: I was already discipling people in the early mornings, over lunches, even at my house after my kids went to bed. But I also knew that saying no to God wasn't acceptable. How can I turn down God's answers to my prayers because I'm "too busy"?

I sensed God echoing a similar question back to me that I had asked the church planter just a few months before: "If I sent you ten hungry leaders tomorrow, what would you do with them?" I had no good answer.

My realization: I was the bottleneck to my own prayers. My desire to disciple others, to equip everyday folks to join God's work, was clouded by unsustainability. My systems were maxed out. I either needed to change my systems or change my prayers.

When our paradigms shift or even bust, God goes to work on us. People who have lost fifty pounds will tell you about the moment they looked in the mirror and had a wake-up call. When my friend almost died in a motor-cycle accident, he realized how selfishly he had been living. Billionaires hit a moment where they have no idea what to do with all the money they have been sprinting after. Such points of holy frustration and deep wrestling beckon us to reexamine our lives. They leave us utterly humbled. They remind us that we have limits even as they provide fuel for the fire of the Divine.

Perhaps you are experiencing one of these moments right now or sense that you are heading toward one. These moments leave us feeling helpless, but they ripen us for change.

My crisis moment forced me to find a framework to lean back on. It wasn't out of my own brilliance; it didn't come to me in my favorite coffee shop, on a spiritual retreat, or on a 14,000-foot Colorado peak. God forced my hand, and then he pointed me toward the most freedom I have ever experienced as a minister of the gospel. I found a process where I could work smarter, not harder, to help unleash God's people around me. I have never experienced this kind of fruit before with so little weight on me and such immediate reproducibility. These principles formed a simple grid to engage hungry leaders, and it has made all the difference.

LIVING IN THE TENSION

In Acts 6 we are given a front-row seat into a crisis moment in the early church. The viral, grassroots movement of "the Way" was thriving. The church seemed to be capable of taking over the world as it expanded—until now. Now there was conflict, and as church leaders rubbed up against it, they realized more of the same was not going to work.

Now in these days when the disciples were increasing in number, a complaint by the Hellenists arose against the Hebrews because their widows were being neglected in the daily distribution. And the twelve summoned the full number of the disciples

and said, "It is not right that we should give up
preaching the word of God to serve tables."
ACTS 6:1-2

What was the issue here?

- They needed to preach the Word.
- They needed to meet tangible needs.
- Their existing systems could no longer serve both.

So they came up with a great plan in the tension of this moment.

"Therefore, brothers, pick out from among you
seven men of good repute, full of the Spirit and
of wisdom, whom we will appoint to this duty.
But we will devote ourselves to prayer and to the
ministry of the word." And what they said pleased
the whole gathering, and they chose Stephen, a man
full of faith and of the Holy Spirit, and Philip, and
Prochorus, and Nicanor, and Timon, and Parmenas,
and Nicolaus, a proselyte of Antioch. These they set
before the apostles, and they prayed and laid their
hands on them.
ACTS 6:3-6

In the midst of great momentum, beautiful chaos had
been building. To sustain their momentum, the apostles
created a new structure. The result was explosive: "And the
word of God continued to increase, and the number of the

disciples multiplied greatly in Jerusalem, and a great many of the priests became obedient to the faith" (Acts 6:7). Many more people came to faith, and they reached a new, strategic subgroup of people: Jewish priests who came to faith in Christ, validating their message to the broader community.

Thanks to the introduction of *structure,* the church in Jerusalem continued to grow, and the gospel continued to multiply into other hubs, eventually spreading all over the world! What Christian leader doesn't want to be part of something like that?

Most church leaders I interact with aren't good buddies with structure. In fact, for some, *structure* feels like a four-letter word. It sounds foreign, crusty, even unspiritual. Forming systems feels like wrestling a muddy pig to the ground—neither fun nor easy. I have never met one person who got into full-time ministry because they dreamed of creating new structures. It's about the people.

But structure is vital to loving people. When we are faithful to obey God, we bear fruit, and when that fruit exceeds our systems, we must expand—and our expansion itself must be faithful.

Too many people naively think that structure is the enemy of movement, when really structure can be the missing link. Sometimes our avoidance of structure is simply a convenient excuse to do things ourselves or avoid hard work.

KINGDOM MOVEMENT

Dee Hock, the founder of the Visa credit card association, coined the term *chaordic* to describe the mixing of chaos and order. As it happens, chaos and order often coexist in nature. Their combination in the world is typically strikingly beautiful.[1] Hock suggests this can be applied to human organizations—which would include the church.

For most people, movement = chaos. Think about the fear that social movements and radicalism strike into governments. And yet it seems as though followers of Jesus everywhere are praying and laboring more and more toward a movement. They see the chaos of change as evidence of a movement brewing. There is a holy urgency in the air.

I am lucky enough to intersect with people living with this holy urgency. I prayer-walk with church planters who feel a deep call to reclaim the forgotten ground beneath their feet and take spiritual responsibility for their parishes. A friend of mine owns a café and intentionally uses it as a place to connect with people far from God and create places where people can be known. An aging church gave their building away to a church plant that was only half a year old so the neighborhood could be reached again. A couple heading toward retirement paved the way for a church in their community by asking, "What does God want to do in this town?" Every other month I gather for a roundtable with a group of Kingdom-hearted leaders who want nothing more than to see God's Kingdom advancing from Colorado's Front Range to the ends of the earth.

What actualizes this holy urgency? In his book *Movements That Change the World*, Steve Addison highlights the life of John Wesley as an example of how great movements happen.

His goal was to establish a movement of people who were learning to obey Christ and to walk as he did. . . .

Wesley was not interested in just attracting crowds. What set Wesley apart was not the gospel he preached but his ability to gather converts into a disciplined movement. . . . As a brilliant strategist and innovator, he created and adapted structures that strengthened and united his followers, while facilitating the movement's rapid expansion.[2]

Most people think *disciplined* and *movement* don't go together any more than *structured* and *chaos*. But while it's easy to picture John Wesley as a blazing visionary drawing crowds to himself by sheer charisma, it was the discipline of creating structure that turned converts into movement makers.

Living in Colorado, I drive on a lot of mountain roads. Many of them are downright scary. I rarely notice guardrails on level ground, but they are pretty comforting on those high mountain roads. Guardrails aren't just for icy roads and emergencies. They give you a frame of reference and allow you to relax a bit, knowing that you won't take a cliff dive. Guardrails are rarely used, but when you brush them you are really thankful they're there.

Movements are birthed in the heart of God, but guardrails are constructed by wise leaders. The best guardrails are informed by biblical principles and take the shape of an adaptable ministry model: We set up appropriate structures, as we saw in Acts 6, so as many people as possible can participate fully in the family and mission of God.

We must not confuse guardrails with roadblocks. Roadblocks stop forward momentum. Guardrails are different: They exist to help forward movement happen safely and efficiently. Perhaps you have accidentally contributed to a culture of blocking roads toward gospel expansion.

People used to refer to Colorado's Front Range as a "church planters' graveyard." Loads of church planters had parachuted into our region, only to close up shop after a short time. I have heard similar names thrown out all over the country. I kept hearing this phrase, and I couldn't shake it. Eventually, I was tasked with modifying how our church supported church planters. After praying for a few months, devouring a few church-planting books, and having a few too many late-night conversations with church planters, I thought God might be calling us out of the graveyard to another city, more convenient and exciting than my own. After praying over my "desired" place to plant, however, my wife and I recognized it as a figment of my own desire. Turns out it was more about escape than calling. It also turns out my wife is more in tune with the Holy Spirit than I am. I was more confused than ever. In the drive back to my city in our shaky Saturn, I knew it was time to transition from living in my city to making it our home. (I write more about fighting escapism and "the grass is greener in another place" ideology in my book *Staying Is the New Going*.)

After prayer, wise counsel, and confirmation from others, I realized we needed a different process for church planting in our area. While success in the eyes of others does not necessarily equate to faithfulness, I knew we could find different ways to help church start-ups be more effective. My wife and I sensed the call to stay put and "plant" a church-planting hub right in the church planters' graveyard.

There is a desperate need for new churches to "live the gospel into" the places they are planting among the people God has placed them around. God does unique things in every place, and we must learn to respect our own place by taking into account the events, traditions, rhythms, food, celebrations, and language of those who reside there.

Today, when the people we train through Frontline Church Planting leave us at the end of their apprenticeships and residencies for their next season of life and ministry, they do so armed with these lasting principles. The principle of *contextualizing the gospel* has become a guardrail for their ministries, informing their model of ministry wherever they go, so that they discover God's work in a place rather than imposing a church on it. One of our church-planting residents had come from Puerto Rico. When he realized the barriers to launching a church gathering among traditionally Catholic Hispanics, he began making adjustments to his strategy. His commitment to a place and its people became a guardrail for his ministry.

We all need to develop a ministry model, but we cannot rely on it. We are far too skilled at planting churches in our heads and reaching people we've never actually met. A model generally works for a limited time in a limited environment. What began as good contextualization can easily become a crutch to lean on. Models become cemented and regulated like roadblocks. But principles can be applied across contexts. No program can teach every skill, every response, every nugget of wisdom or every biblical truth needed in church leadership. The best preparation for ministry is a simple framework, clear principles, and a learned ability to trust the leading of the Spirit.

PRAY, OBEY, SAY, GET OUT OF THE WAY

It certainly is possible to overstructure and kill momentum before it starts. Many denominations started as thriving, viral movements; over time they added levels of bureaucracy, and their momentum slowed. Some churches are experiencing the same thing. Nearly every denomination with which I have come in contact in the last few years is rapidly recalibrating to address this drag and recover their momentum. Some of the shifts are incredibly exciting!

But most of the church and ministry leaders I know don't struggle with overstructuring. They're entrepreneurial and apostolic; they revel in the pregnant possibility that attends chaos. In the same way that overstructured organizations need to free up room for new ideas that will allow expansion and new movement, understructured leaders need to prepare themselves to keep their momentum from degenerating into chaos.

The following mantra has been a good organizing tool for me: If we are going to multiply our impact and keep in step with God's Kingdom movement, we must *pray, obey, say,* and *get out of the way.*

Pray for a movement. Jesus teaches his disciples to pray, "Your kingdom come, your will be done, on earth as it is in heaven" (Matthew 6:10). This sets our eyes on a bigger story than our little lives. Prayer paves the way for a movement by readying our hearts and aligning with God. Whether you are pursuing the great commission in your suburban neighborhood, within medical clinics in Ghana, or among your friends who don't know Jesus, prayer comes first.

I find it helpful, as I pray the Lord's Prayer, to replace the word *earth* with the name of my region, state, city, neighborhood, or local gathering spot. I pray for God's Kingdom to come in the Northglen neighborhood as I picture Rick, Ray, Gina, and Eric, who live just steps from my front door. As I pray over my neighborhood in this way, I begin to see the cracks in the spiritual foundations, and God challenges me and my family to fill those cracks with the mortar of the gospel. When we pray for his Kingdom, God will open our eyes to the brokenness that exists around us, and the opportunities for heaven to come to earth.

A life of prayer doesn't happen accidentally. Open up your calendar and schedule a time to actively pray. Perhaps you can find a high point in your city where you can look over the sprawl of your place and pray for gospel movement there. I'm a little squirmy, so I love prayer-walking a neighborhood or campus to pray for God's Kingdom to rule in the beauty and brokenness of that place.

Perhaps coffee shop prayers are more your style. A friend of mine is in the habit of waiting fifteen minutes after sitting down with his cup of coffee to pull out his phone or computer so he can take that time to pray for those in the shop. In any case, perhaps it's time to take your prayer time out of your prayer closet.

Obey Kingdom impulses. I've never met anyone who claimed the kingdom of this earth isn't busted. I've also never met anyone who didn't want to be part of righting wrongs and changing the world. When we obey the prodding of the Holy Spirit and sense God's Kingdom impulses, others will follow. In the same way that microbusinesses participate in a broader economy, each and every follower of Jesus functions as a priest with authority in God's upside-down Kingdom (Revelation 1:5-6). God's people, working in different spheres of a place, form a Kingdom ecosystem.

When we commit ourselves in advance to obey God's Kingdom impulses, we ready ourselves to be used by God. Words are cheap, but action will cost you. People are skeptical and noncommittal today. We live in a "maybe" culture where we ironically struggle to commit to the right things while chronically battling overcommitment. As your family, your small group, or your church takes new risks to obey God, others will get the courage to follow God in ways that seemed crazy in the past. Maybe the ideas *are* crazy, but people will be emboldened when they see others crazy enough to obey God. The Kingdom ecosystem flourishes when God's people obey Kingdom impulses.

Recall a time you felt led or directed by the Holy Spirit to do something uncomfortable. What was the experience like? What would make you more receptive to similar impulses in the future?

Say what God is up to. I believe every human is tuned in to the rhythm of God's Kingdom. People are trying to make sense of these God impulses, even if they don't know it. Don't try to generate Kingdom work; try to uncover it.

One of the major roles of every spiritual leader is telling what God is doing in our lives and the lives of others. This kind of storytelling is deeply powerful. It validates small victories, assigns meaning to challenges and losses, and inspires people to dream. Story unlocks our heart, shocks our imagination, and activates our faith. Unearthing and celebrating God's work in those around us is one of the greatest investments spiritual leaders can make.

Each Kingdom story births more stories. By celebrating the Kingdom obedience of others, the stories we tell give people permission to participate in God's larger narrative. We must become winsome storytellers of the Kingdom coming around us.

If you want your church to be more mission-minded, evangelistic, or welcoming, don't just preach it from the front. Take some time to reflect on others who are practicing simple obedience. Think through the appropriate venues where you can tell these stories and celebrate the work that God is doing through them. Flank your preaching with stories of ordinary heroes among you who are taking Jesus seriously.

Get out of the way. This is the hardest one for me. Sometimes we, as leaders, are the bottleneck—at times, even the roadblock. God seems to be developing amazing things in front of us, and our flesh pushes us to take credit. At some point the people you lead need to move beyond you and take responsibility for their own ministry. God, not you, is the master networker and connector.

While our souls long for a movement, our flesh grabs for control, power, and validation. Every follower of Jesus has great possibility—God-given genius—but we also have the capacity to get in the way. If we are living in the way of Jesus, we are servants. As we humbly recognize our role, we must be ready to get out of the way at the right time.

While it can be painful to get out of the way, it's even more fulfilling to hear the stories that come out of people's unique pursuit of Kingdom movement. Kingdom leaders must recognize when their presence in a relationship or ministry is a hindrance. We need to practice what we preach about the priesthood of all believers.

Spend some time thinking through a few areas where you need to get out of the way. Write down the names of a few leaders who might need you to get out of the way in order for them to rise to their full potential.

In order to see a sustained multiplication of disciples, we need a mix of structure and chaos, of method and madness. We need the disciplines of praying, obeying, and saying, along with the humility of getting out of the way. When I was seeking to multiply disciples and leaders with no guardrails, I felt out of control and exhausted. When God met me that day in my helplessness, he gave me the gift of structure. This has helped me to organize the chaos that comes with momentum, so I can better see and respond to what God is doing without limiting the creativity of God's people. Jesus has already launched his movement; his Spirit is continually propelling it forward. We are invited to join in, commanded against stifling or squelching it, but privileged to do our part to sustain it.

DISCUSSION QUESTIONS

Recall a time you obeyed the Holy Spirit and did something uncomfortable. What was the result?

What unique expression of prayer will you make a habit in your life?

What recent stories come to mind of others you know living in obedience to God? How can you tell those stories?

Which areas of leadership or ministry do you need to step away from? Whom might God want to raise up in your place?

2
THE KINGDOM

We become what we adore.
SAINT AUGUSTINE

*In every seed is the potential for a tree, and in every tree is the potential
for a forest. But the potential is all contained in the initial seed.*
ALAN HIRSCH

The kingdom of God does not consist in talk but in power.
1 CORINTHIANS 4:20

ONE OF THE NEWEST THINGS happening in my city isn't
new at all. It's an old school that nearly got the wrecking
ball. Ivywild School was built in the 1930s as the kind of
elementary school you see in the movies. It has big front
steps, symmetrical sides, and one simple hallway. It's iconic.
But as people moved out of the surrounding neighborhood,
heading for newer homes in safer areas, the school struggled
and was eventually decommissioned. For a few years it sat
unused, overgrown with weeds.

In a beautiful turn of events, local entrepreneurs and
community advocates began to dream about how this building could become a hub for the community. Today Ivywild

School is home to a co-working space, a coffee shop, a bakery, a brewery, event spaces, a concert venue, a farmers' market, and an engineering firm. A church plant even gathers for worship on Sundays in the brewery's barrel aging room. Posters remind you not to miss the next concert, to buy local, and to participate in a slew of community-centered events.

When people walk up the large steps into Ivywild School, they come alive. I will never forget watching two older ladies walk in with amazement. One of them said, "I couldn't stand the thought of them tearing down the school I taught in for so many years." Something that had become worthless to the city is now the pride of the neighborhood.

This story is one that reeks of Kingdom logic, of rags to riches and death to life. It's an upside-down narrative that people will always cheer for.

The upside-down Kingdom of God both amazes and perplexes me. It whispers a simple yet mysterious story—an alternative story to the tired kingdom of this world. Jesus' church, the family of God, must live a different narrative in this consumer-driven, me-first, get-ahead, and "stick it to the man" world we live in. Karl Barth says that the church "exists . . . to set up in the world a new sign which is radically dissimilar to [the world's] own manner and which contradicts it in a way which is full of promise."[1] The church is not perfect, but she should be strikingly different from the patterns of this world.

The Kingdom of God is foundational to our lives. It changes everything. It should also be foundational to any ministry we participate in and is the best place to start any discipleship process. Any other foundation sends us slowly drifting into the riptide of self and crashing onto the rocks of our own tiny kingdoms.

Kingdom theology has often been overlooked. Perhaps it doesn't offer accelerated solutions in a world of quick fixes. Perhaps acknowledging God's centrality in all things renders us helpless in a self-help culture. Perhaps living an alternative story is simply too risky. Yet Kingdom theology is not just where we should start our ministry; it's where Jesus started his. If Jesus started his ministry heralding a new Kingdom, so should we. The Kingdom of God provides both focus and breadth for training new believers and retraining seasoned leaders.

The Kingdom has been undervalued, undertaught, and under-understood in our churches. A friend of mine told me that the first time someone taught him about the Kingdom of God, he was mad. As he looked over Scripture with new, Kingdom lenses, he wondered, *If this is such a big deal, why has no one ever told me about it?* As for me, after years of sermons, Bible studies, leadership groups, and ministry roles, no one explained the centrality of the Kingdom of God to me. It was as if my eyes were veiled. Then suddenly, I saw it laced throughout Scripture.

The Kingdom of God is the primary message of John the Baptist, Jesus, and Paul. *John the Baptist* tilled the soil by announcing it, "preaching in the wilderness of Judea, 'Repent, for the kingdom of heaven is at hand'" (Matthew 3:1-2). John was a man of the wilderness with a message and a megaphone, a forerunner tasked with getting people ready for someone great. That wasn't just a message of a new king but the counterintuitive Kingdom he would establish.

Jesus began and ended his ministry proclaiming the Kingdom. Before he even recruited the disciples to be part of his team, he was declaring the Kingdom: "Repent, for the kingdom of heaven is at hand" (Matthew 4:17). The Kingdom was highlighted in every word and action of his ministry: "Jesus went throughout all the cities and villages, teaching in their synagogues and proclaiming the gospel of the kingdom and healing every disease and every affliction" (Matthew 9:35).

Jesus challenged others to proclaim the Kingdom even when it inconveniently interrupted their lives (see Luke 9:60). And after being raised from the dead, Jesus spent a season reinforcing his Kingdom message, "appearing to them during forty days and speaking about the kingdom of God" (Acts 1:3). It was the last course he would teach from earth.

Paul spent months debating the Kingdom. Much of his time and energy in Ephesus was spent proclaiming the Kingdom of God and persuading others about it. "For three months [he] spoke boldly, reasoning and persuading them about the kingdom of God" (Acts 19:8). This season of Kingdom proclamation would lead to all of Asia Minor hearing the message of the gospel (Acts 19:10). The Kingdom was a recurring theme throughout his ministry and his letters.

The Kingdom of God is something we simply can't afford to miss. Once you start to grasp it, your life and ministry will never be the same.

WHAT IS THE KINGDOM OF GOD?

Simply put, the Kingdom of God is his reign and rule in all things. As Jesus modeled to us, we are invited to proclaim and embody that God is on his throne. Neither words nor actions alone are sufficient.

God's alternative Kingdom story is an upside-down way of life. In God's reign the last become first, misfits are welcomed in, prejudice is crushed, old things are made new, busted things become beautiful, grace trumps works, dependence yields freedom, to die is gain, and people rejoice when they fall short. When I discuss these conundrums with others, I find they resonate deep in the human soul. Every human soul is longing for redemption. The Gospels fascinate people of all faith preferences because in nearly every situation Jesus turns the world on its head. We all want to live in such realities.

And yet, because it remains a mystery, talk of the Kingdom can easily lead to confusion. One such confusion is the difference between the Kingdom of God and heaven. Although sometimes referred to as "the kingdom of heaven," the Kingdom is something we experience today, as we recognize God's reign and rule over our lives. Heaven is different— a place those who call upon Jesus will eventually experience. As Shane Claiborne and Jonathan Wilson-Hartgrove write, "The kingdom is not some place that our souls are taken away to when we die. It is, instead, an order that comes to earth—right here among us who call ourselves daughters and sons of God."[2] God beckons us to be part of his Kingdom work right now. Robert Webber and Rodney Clapp remind us, "In Jesus the future has invaded the present. The kingdom of God has begun."[3]

So the Kingdom of heaven is not heaven. Neither is the Kingdom a synonym for the church. As members of the family of God, we are to help the world taste and see the glory of God's Kingdom, but we are not the fullness of it. When we live like Jesus, embodying how he lived, we surrender to a new reign and rule, one that feels upside down and inside out. As the church, God's deeply loved family, we are to bring heaven to earth. When we proclaim and embody his Kingdom we are declaring that God is at work, publicly and secretly, and that his fingerprints are all over our lives, neighborhoods, cities, and world. We remind a depressed world that has been emptied of meaning that there is, indeed, reason for joy again.

OBSTACLES TO EXPERIENCING THE KINGDOM

This might be your first time grappling with the meaning of the Kingdom of God. Or perhaps you've grasped the Kingdom for years. Maybe you always heard it in the distant background like the safety talk before your plane takes off. Whatever your vantage point, the Kingdom of God deserves careful consideration because it's foundational to our ministry—the ultimate guardrail for our movement. Here are a few mentalities we need to constantly guard against.

Our kingdom-come mentality. Jesus taught his disciples to pray, "Your kingdom come" (Luke 11:2). This prayer serves as a check against a common impulse to build our own little kingdoms for ourselves. We often see churches having turf wars, fighting for neighborhood territory as if they are warring gangs. These competitions are not reflective of the Kingdom of God; they reflect a mentality of constructing tiny kingdoms we must protect.

A similar fear can lead us to hoard the resources God has given us, instead of making them available to our neighbors (and neighboring churches) in need. This fear can rear its ugly head in the form of self-promotion instead of self-sacrifice, pride instead of humility. It's this mentality that leads to new church planters getting the cold shoulder from established churches instead of the warm welcome of gospel partnership.

When we live by God's Kingdom ethic, arms are outstretched to give freely to those who are in need. There are few things greater than the prayers and generosity that church planters experience from other churches and groups within a city. Very few things sow these kinds of Kingdom seeds.

Surety-then-faith mentality. In the Sermon on the Mount Jesus instructs the crowd to "seek first the kingdom of God and his righteousness, and all these things will be added to you" (Matthew 6:33). We have a very realistic need for money, clothes, and food, and we like to control our path to get these. Often our prayers are only as big as our physical needs or maybe even our wants. But the Kingdom of God is the acknowledgment of the rule and reign of God in our lives; it prioritizes our obedience to God and reflection of the character of God over our needs. It assumes (with faith) that our needs will be met by a sovereign God. We often acknowledge that God is our provider but go on living as though we are wandering the streets on our own. We can easily bow to the idol of security. This is often evidenced when we claim we will be generous if God provides excess. It just doesn't work that way. Earthly surety cannot coexist with faith.

The poverty mentality. Poverty makes people obsessed with the present moment. Poverty eliminates future vision because the needs of the moment are screaming too loudly. As the old adage goes: "Don't ask a man what he wants for dinner when he's drowning."

Spiritual poverty is different from physical poverty. Spiritual poverty leads us toward grabbing for spare change instead of living in the riches of God's love. Spiritually speaking, disciples of Jesus live in abundance. Jesus' Kingdom message was received by the poor and marginalized but rejected by the wealthy and powerful. Similarly, throughout the Scriptures are juxtapositions of material wealth and poverty, as well as spiritual poverty versus riches. Why is that? It's the luxury of the wealthy and powerful to look beyond the moment, but the side effect is that they also look beyond gratitude for God's goodness.

You are likely rich in the eyes of this world if you were able to afford this book. Those who are rich in wealth are often spiritually poor, laboring to build their own kingdoms instead of acknowledging God's Kingdom.

A culture of spiritual poverty is the antithesis of a Kingdom life. "If I only had a little more" cannot be the cry of God's children living a Kingdom life. We won't see the work God is doing beyond us when we are too busy scrambling to gather more around us.

PARTICIPATING IN GOD'S KINGDOM

Perhaps the saddest thing I see happening today is people who are leaving God's church in search of God's Kingdom. While I understand the cultural shifts and religious migration patterns away from the church, it grieves me. Ordinary radicals, hipsters, soccer moms, elementary school kids, bloggers, and high school students are raising awareness of atrocities such as sex trafficking, child abuse, and child soldiers. A few years ago, I was speaking to an auditorium full of students. I took a quick survey of how many of them owned a pair of Toms shoes, made by the company that donates a pair of shoes to a child in need for every pair purchased. Eighty percent of the room raised their hands. We cannot even buy a pair of shoes today without thinking about the impact our choices have on others.

But more often than not, even those Christians involved in such acts of compassion and works of justice are going outside the church to do so. People want to wrap their lives around something that matters. Little people want to leave a big impact, and most people aren't being offered an opportunity to do so in the church. Our churches must allow people to do that!

Something is wrong if you look around your life and your church and nothing is propelled outward into the lives of others. Jesus talked about justice before it was popular, and he actively went about filling the cracks in our world with the mortar of the gospel. In a world driven by causes and activism, churches simply can't afford to pray prayers and do ministries that are limited to the size of their congregation.

This season of causes and advocacy in our world could be a great opportunity for the church. The movement of God is taking place subtly in homes, neighborhoods, prayer closets, cafés, art galleries, tattoo parlors, and yes, church gatherings. No need to try to start a movement; just join one.

While living in our house the first year, we noticed a crack in our neighborhood. Longtime neighbors and parents from the school across the street were coexisting, but there was no connection. They would pass one another with an awkward smile or a wave. As my wife and I dreamed about serving our neighbors, we settled on the idea of serving coffee every Friday to school parents across from the school. "Free Coffee Friday" was greeted with generosity and enthusiasm. People have offered to help in different ways. For the last five years, every Friday when school is in session, exhausted parents (us included), bus drivers, neighbors, and school officials have gathered on the corner to experience a small piece of heaven coming to earth.

Not only do people want to experience things being made whole, they want to participate in the process. That's because we were made for life in God's Kingdom, and something in us is brought to life when we encounter it. Everyone senses a Kingdom impulse, even those who don't know Jesus. Look around you, and you'll see others seeking out wholeness and restoration in their relationships, neighborhood, and city.

FRUIT TREES VERSUS SEED BUCKETS

I took up gardening a few years ago. I went to Rick's Garden Center near my home and cluelessly flipped through packets of seeds. They were locked in their packets, dry and lonely yet full of potential.

Even I was able to figure out gardening. Turns out that it's pretty simple. The bright Colorado days provided the sunlight, and at night I watered the ground, trusting that something was activating below the surface. The seeds became plants, and when the plants were ready they burst through the ground. We enjoyed some fresh salads and tasty salsa that summer.

Those packets of seeds produced a great crop that first year, but if they had stayed in the packets, they would have produced nothing.

Jesus describes the Kingdom as a seed meant to be planted and multiplied (Matthew 13). Every disciple, Jesus suggests, carries the seed of the Kingdom with them. When the right elements are in place, those seeds are activated, producing beautiful and fruitful results.

Unfortunately, many of our churches look less like thriving gardens and more like buckets full of seeds—outposts of unrealized Kingdom potential. Any Kingdom movement is stifled by oppressive structure or, on the flip side, an accommodation of unstructured chaos. People are waiting to be released into our world with the great hope they have been given in Christ. At its core, a dynamic Kingdom movement is really pretty simple: We add obedience to the seed of the Kingdom in us, and God activates those tiny seeds into thriving gardens. God's Kingdom has come, and joy has come with it.

DISCUSSION QUESTIONS

In what distinct ways can you see God's Kingdom coming around you?

Which of the three obstacles to the Kingdom do you most easily fall into—our kingdom-come mentality, surety-then-faith mentality, or poverty mentality?

How are you helping others to experience the Kingdom of God?

Does your church resemble fruit groves or seed buckets? What needs to happen for your church to yield a harvest?

3

THE GREAT COMMISSION

A disciple-led movement is one in which the church equips and lets loose the disciples within the church to the community.
KEVIN PALAU

I've found that a church which correctly applies the concept of true discipleship will accomplish both goals: growth and depth.
ED STETZER

To be a disciple is to be a disciple-maker.
COLIN MARSHALL

THE WORD *MISSION* is everywhere today. Organizations tout their mission statements on their home page. Pastors describe their congregation as missional. Seminaries proudly state they are producing mission-minded thinkers. Mission is starting to feel like a buzzword.

Most of us would say we want to be missional Christians. It implies that we want a life of action. We want to emulate the mission of Jesus in our lives and in our churches. We believe that this message, the great gospel of Jesus, is the best thing on earth. I am grateful for how the missional conversation has led thousands of people to reimagine how the church can regain a missionary posture in their communities and an incarnational presence in their neighborhoods.

Missional, however, has become a victim of its own buzz. It has become a style of church, a basis for conferences, and a branding tool. Its meaning has become confused. If missional people are to be marked by mission, then we must clarify what our mission actually is.

Jesus gave us a clear articulation of our mission: Plain and simple, our mission is to make disciples (Matthew 28:18-19). I believe every church mission statement should simply be a fresh retelling of this instruction from Jesus.

If our way of "going missional" doesn't involve making disciples, then it isn't missional at all. Jesus was on a mission, but the method of his mission was *incarnation.*

When I released my book *Staying Is the New Going,* I found myself invited to talk about its themes of growing roots and staying long enough in a place for lives of mission to deeply impact those around us. I will be honest—I would sometimes get discouraged as I looked around. Long after the conferences were over, the books were underlined, and the tweets were retweeted, I'd find myself asking this sinking question: *Who is actually making disciples?* Where are all the disciples who are making disciples?

As followers of Jesus, we are the only ones sent with this specific and world-changing mission. Christians are not unique in their concern about sex trafficking. Many non-Christians adopt children from struggling nations. Most people I know have compassion for drug addicts. Lots of folks host block parties with their neighbors, collect money for charity, hand out food at the park, tutor underprivileged kids in struggling elementary schools, and "like" a plethora of causes on Facebook. Those all around us recognize that this earth has a lot of cracks and could be in a whole lot better shape. All kinds of people do great things. But only the people of God have such a potent reason *why*.

In his book *Start with Why*, Simon Sinek contends that an organization's mission "starts from the inside out": "It all starts with Why. . . . By WHY I mean what is your purpose, cause or belief? WHY does your company exist? WHY do you get out of bed every morning? And WHY should anyone care? . . . We rarely say WHY we do WHAT we do."[1]

Our why is another guardrail for our movement. We do what we do because Jesus, the one we love, has beckoned us to do so. Jesus told us to help convey the best news ever. The most missional thing we can do is carry on Jesus' work in the world, and ask others to join us in this mission.

SEVEN SIMPLE TRUTHS

Try to imagine you are one of the original disciples. You have given up your life to join this ragtag bunch. You're all-in, with no backup plan. You have seen and done amazing things in the name of Jesus. Then Jesus dies, and shortly after that earthshaking heartbreak you hear rumors that he has been raised from the dead. And then you actually see him again. Imagine hearing these words:

> All authority in heaven and on earth has been given
> to me. Go therefore and make disciples of all nations,
> baptizing them in the name of the Father and of the
> Son and of the Holy Spirit, teaching them to observe

all that I have commanded you. And behold, I am
with you always, to the end of the age.

MATTHEW 28:18-20

We remember these words as the great commission. Seven
simple truths emerge from it.

- *We have been given authority.* "All authority in heaven
  and on earth has been given to me."
- *We have a new purpose.* "Go therefore . . ."
- *We are tasked with making disciples.* "Make disciples of
  all nations . . ."
- *We are tasked with preparing the way for physical and
  spiritual baptism.* "Baptizing them . . ."
- *We are tasked with sharing about Jesus, his Father, and
  the Holy Spirit.* "In the name of the Father and of the
  Son and of the Holy Spirit . . ."
- *We are tasked with teaching others about the life and
  commands of Christ.* "Teaching them to observe all
  that I have commanded you."
- *We aren't alone, because the Spirit of God goes with us.*
  "And behold, I am with you always, to the end of
  the age."

Talk about empowering! It reminds me of when my dad
would leave for a business trip. He would tell me I had more
responsibility while he was away: I was to take good care of
my mom and protect the family. I was "on duty." My little

chest filled up, and all sixty pounds of me was ready to take out bandits and dragons with a pool noodle.

In a similar way, Jesus has passed the torch to every follower of Jesus. We've been commanded to go make disciples, and we are given seven specific directives to clarify what that entails.

More than that, Scripture describes what making disciples looks like. Throughout the Gospels, discipleship was both taught and caught. Our mission is to make disciples. That's what missional people do.

FACE TO FACE

I have four very active kids. Sometimes our house feels like an overcrowded animal shelter. At times we all get overwhelmed by the pure chaos of living in a loud family of six. When one of my kids gets overwhelmed by the madness of it all, I take them aside for what I call "face-to-face." I bend down, touch my nose to theirs, calm them down, and give them instructions. They proceed with a bit more composure.

I believe that most of us are overstimulated by stressful lives in a crazy world and have simply lost our focus. We find ourselves pulled in a thousand different directions. We are in need of a "face-to-face" refocusing moment with the Father. In these moments God can remind us what actually matters.

I work with a lot of churches, and I have observed that most churches are overstimulated and have lost focus on the task at hand. They don't know what they're aiming at, so they aim at everything. Lacking focus leads to husky and high-maintenance structures and programs. Every follower of Jesus can get caught up in simply doing life, and every church can get caught up in simply "doing church." Even pastors can skirt around Jesus' commission.

Most churches need a shift in mission from "doing church" to making disciples. You might be able to cut out half the activities in your life and half the programs in your church and become more fruitful. When people comprehend that they are called by Jesus to make disciples, and when leaders take responsibility for empowering people to make disciples, then churches get healthy.

There's a man named Tony in our church who embodies what it means to be a discipler. Tony leads discipleship groups with guys who have just been baptized and guys who have been in church their whole lives. Some of the men who are elders in our church have matured because Tony stepped into their lives and challenged them to lead their own group. I know Tony lives "face-to-face" with the Father because he remains laser-focused on discipleship. He owns a flower business that keeps him very busy, but there is always time for early-morning or -evening discipleship groups. Over the years he has even turned down formal leadership positions so that he can stay focused on leading these discipleship groups. We need more leaders like Tony who will commit their time and energy to making disciples who make disciples.

Making disciples is the foundation for healthy Christian leadership. It should form the basis for our small groups, missionary endeavors, neighborhood ministry, church planting, and pastoring. If we have no process for making disciples, then the rest of our ministry processes will never fully mature. The late Dallas Willard was very clear about discipleship. "Every church needs to be able to answer two questions. One, do we have a plan for making disciples? Two, does our plan work?"[2]

Amidst the chaos of life, we must remain focused on our Father's desire for more disciples to be formed. We do that by focusing on three key dimensions of making disciples. I define a disciple as one who is learning Jesus, seeking to obey him, and reproducing his life.

LEARNING JESUS

The desire to learn is the start to becoming a disciple. There is no substitute for the hunger that drives us to learn. "If you abide in my word, you are truly my disciples, and you will know the truth, and the truth will set you free" (John 8:31-32). Learning the ins and outs of the life of Jesus is the first step toward discipleship. This encompasses what Jesus did and what Jesus told us to do. During Jesus' ministry he gave roughly fifty commands for us to go and do likewise.

Start teaching about life in Christ through the life of Christ. Sometimes we've skipped right over the life of Jesus because his words and actions have become tragically familiar to us. Robert Webber and Rodney Clapp write,

> American Christians know Jesus too well. His parables are like old jokes to them—the tired punchlines are memorized, so why hear them again? . . . But in first-century Palestine there was no such

attitude. The parables were baffling and astonishing. The deeds were shocking.[3]

Let's not forget how counterintuitive and shocking Jesus' life was. We must expose others to the life of Jesus if we hope to see them formed by Jesus. John's Gospel is a great place to start exploring with a curious or hungry friend.

As soon as someone comes to faith in Jesus or expresses a desire to truly grow as a disciple, we must center them on the life and commands of Christ. C. S. Lewis expressed the centrality of this:

> The Church exists for nothing else but to draw men into Christ, to make them little Christs. If they are not doing that, all the cathedrals, clergy, missions, sermons, even the Bible itself, are simply a waste of time. God became Man for no other purpose.[4]

All our Christian activity—all the book studies, worship nights, service to the community, care for the homeless, love for our neighbors, and mission trips in the world—it doesn't matter if we aren't shaping our lives after how Jesus lived. Apart from Christ these things turn into empty emotion, legalism, or mere community service. I can only imagine how our churches would be transformed if we saw ourselves as "little Christs" obsessed with loving God and loving others. If people don't have a model for who they are to become, how do we expect them to become disciples?

As you learn to live of Jesus, you will see that he desired

more than cognition and repetition. Jesus demanded obedience from his disciples:

> Why do you call me "Lord, Lord," and not do what
> I tell you? Everyone who comes to me and hears my
> words and does them, I will show you what he is
> like: he is like a man building a house, who dug deep
> and laid the foundation on the rock. And when a
> flood arose, the stream broke against that house and
> could not shake it, because it had been well built.
> But the one who hears and does not do them is like
> a man who built a house on the ground without
> a foundation. When the stream broke against it,
> immediately it fell, and the ruin of that house was
> great.
>
> LUKE 6:46-49

I often apply this passage to being a father. Every day my kids have many moments to either obey or disobey. When my kids don't follow through on what I've asked them to do, I feel like saying, "Why do you call me Daddy, Daddy, but don't do what I ask you to do?" When I confront them about not doing what I asked them, they often say, "I know, Daddy, I know." And they're right: They do know. But obedience isn't simply about knowing; it's about responding.

I learned one of my most valuable discipleship lessons in a small group that went up in smoke. My wife and I were invited to join a small group some friends had started. The group decided to study through all the commands of Christ scattered throughout the Gospels. It was a brilliant idea, but it fell short. There was no commitment to the group, so attendance waned and we never finished the study. It was like watching a ship sink slowly while you're tied to the mast. Without sustained commitment, discipleship loses momentum.

We must avoid a major pitfall here. While learning Jesus can propel us into obeying Jesus, we must not simply find ourselves reading from a discipleship checklist. "Complete this list and you will grow" leads us down a rough road. Jesus calls the Pharisees a "brood of vipers" (Matthew 3:7; 12:34; 23:33), and yet their actions were the best in the land. They had a great outer life but no heart for God. Jesus said, "These people honor me with their lips but their hearts are far from me" (Matthew 15:8, NIV). We must guard against missional Pharisaism—a new disguise for an old vice.

Perhaps the structure of your team meetings is actually hindering your disciple-making ministry by simply leading teams into activity. My first role on a church staff was an interim role during college under the senior pastor, a mentor of mine. He would tell us, "We must be the people of God before we do the work of God." I adopted this phrase and have used it ever since. "Being before doing" has literally changed everything about the way I lead teams, but it's still hard to practice. In ministry-team meetings, people tend to show up, pull out their notebook, and want to get down to business. Ministry meetings cannot simply be boardrooms with one spare seat for Jesus. They should feel more like a group of humble learners gathered at the feet of Jesus and ready to yield to the Holy Spirit. I try my very best to start every meeting I lead with a focus on hearts instead of tasks, to treat people as disciples of Jesus, not simply leaders in the church. One of the teams I led always started meetings with dinner, followed by a time of seeking God together. I found that when Scripture and prayer shaped our time together, a few things happened:

- I was more attentive to people's needs—sometimes very weighty ones.
- The team was more collaborative. God brought a spirit of unity that was never about one person, and we submitted to one another.
- We viewed ministry with a heart to see people meet God and experience transformation.
- We gave time to discerning whether the events we were planning were necessary.

I will warn you: Starting meetings as "the people of God" will mess up the "business" you want to accomplish in your ministries. But it's a great mess! Your agenda will become less about planning events or leading a team and more about making disciples. It's amazing how the details end up getting accomplished in the end when we take the risk of being before doing. You can always send e-mails to plan details, but discipleship must be worked out in relationship. Through relational presence at the feet of Jesus, the gospel becomes transformational, changing our allegiance to God and his coming Kingdom.

SEEKING TO OBEY JESUS

We live in a culture that simply does not engage things when we don't feel like it. Our society is marked more by empty emotion and apathy than by obedience and dedication. How many people are exiting churches because they just aren't feeling it?

Once we know the commands of Christ, we choose to either obey them or ignore them. Scripture is pretty clear about the relationship between knowledge of God and obedience.

> Be doers of the word, and not hearers only, deceiving yourselves. For if anyone is a hearer of the word and not a doer, he is like a man who looks intently at his natural face in a mirror. For he looks at himself and goes away and at once forgets what he was like.
>
> JAMES 1:22-24

Those who are truly making disciples are the ones who are hungry for more of God and hungry for life change. They will not be swayed when they are tired or when life becomes mundane. This is not an easy road in an entitled culture that centers around us. Spiritual leadership is not about gaining followers; it's about making disciples.

I have walked alongside leaders dealing with big messes after hiring people whose character and values were overlooked because their résumés were so impressive. I have found that the best thing to look for is *hunger*. Yes, gifting is important, but those who are hungry for God and his Kingdom end up growing a lot in their skills. They are faithful to do the best they can with what they've been given. They ask others to critique them, and they are willing to do anything you ask them to do in order to improve. Their hunger for ministry is born out of their obedience to God's commands.

I grew up in the beautiful state of Virginia. The tall pines in the forest behind my house provided refuge for our forts and protection in our games of cowboys and Indians. For several winters in a row we had intense wind and ice storms. The forest behind my house literally lost half of the trees during a few bad storms. The wind and ice revealed how strong or weak each tree's roots were. It was a logger's dream but a homeowner's nightmare.

This is true in our lives as well. Obedience is tested through the weight of real life struggles, not written exams. You can't "know discipleship." You have to live it. Dietrich Bonhoeffer sums this up beautifully in his book *The Cost of Discipleship*: "Only the obedient believe. If we are to believe, we must obey a concrete command. Without this preliminary step of obedience, our faith will only be pious humbug, and lead us to the grace which is not costly. Everything depends on the first step."[5]

A friend of mine named Austin experienced an uncomfortable call to the first step of obedience. He was reading Matthew 25:40 one night: "Truly, I say to you, as you did it to one of the least of these my brothers, you did it to me." He grappled with the honest thought that he didn't want to feed the hungry, clothe the naked, and house those who slept under the bridge. He pictured Jesus shivering under a bridge and asking for food, while he gave Jesus a dollar and walked away.

Austin was not passionate about helping homeless people, but he recognized that God is. This vision would be the birth of the Acacia Project in downtown Colorado Springs. This ministry still continues today: a group of people committed to obeying Jesus and taking the gospel to those who have been pushed aside and fallen on hard times. They are partnering with several churches and businesses to feed people several times a month, provide clothing and shelter, and allow people who are considered "less than" to have real friends.

The physical needs of the homeless community became so overwhelming that the Acacia Project has created new avenues to share the love of Jesus and focus on the relational and spiritual aspects. They launched a Sunday-morning gathering in a local pizza shop where people could ask questions about God, pray, and open up God's Word. Their faithful presence has been the hands and feet of Jesus to many in our city. We've seen people who live on the streets of Colorado Springs give their lives to Christ, get baptized, and disciple others. One of those men co-leads the ministry today! Not only has the homeless community grown in relationship with Jesus, but God has changed the lives of those who serve the folks who are living on the streets. This is the simple fruit of Austin and a team of people not just knowing God, but seeking to obey him.

REPRODUCING THE LIFE OF JESUS

Discipleship doesn't fully "click" until we impart it to others. In his book *Movements That Change the World,* Steve Addison writes, "Jesus' teaching was obedience oriented. . . . He trained the head, the heart, and the hands of his disciples and expected them to pass on what they learned to others."[6] This process of passing on what we have learned is multiplication. In a tiny seed lies the potential to produce a whole forest.

True discipleship will naturally lead to multiplication. The gospel is the greatest gift this world has ever seen, and it's meant to be given away. Discipling others is spiritual parenthood: We learn to be spiritual mothers and fathers in response to the love of our Father. Healthy churches are full of disciples who make disciples.

Our culture is obsessed with leadership. Just take a glance at the millions of leadership books on Amazon.com. In the church, we must instead be obsessed with discipleship. A disciple is focused on learning and following. Those are the kind of people we want leading others.

Spiritual leaders take others with them toward Jesus and make more disciples. Healthy spiritual leaders who are making disciples around them will help form healthy churches. Jesus spoke of the church in abstract terms, but his clear intention was to leave his work on earth in the feeble yet empowered hands of disciples making disciples, culminating in the church.

Healthy disciples who bring others with them are the spiritual leaders this world needs, and they will form the healthy churches this world needs. We must keep the priority on making disciples.

DISCIPLES ➜ LEADERS ➜ CHURCH
HEALTHY PRIORITIES

The diagram on the previous page shows the development of healthy priorities in the structure of our churches. We don't usually follow this progression in our ministries, however. In fact, things usually develop in the opposite way:

CHURCH → LEADERS → DISCIPLES
MISGUIDED PRIORITIES

Most ministries start with a church-centric view instead of a disciple-centric view. The church planter or new pastor puts full priority on building a church. They scramble to recruit gifted leaders to oversee specific, predetermined ministries. The assumption becomes that once we have every area covered with gifted leaders, we will start making disciples. This "someday" attitude rarely delivers on the expectation. Meanwhile, church leaders feel pressure to have enough cogs in the machine so the team won't burn out. Instead of reproducing disciples, we reproduce leaders of prefab church roles. That's just reality.

The adage "slow down to speed up" is never more true than in leadership development and starting new churches. It takes time and intention to form disciples. There's no way around it. One of my favorite examples of discipleship comes from my friend Bill. He started his college career as a skeptic who found his worth in performance. God rescued him from his life of self, and he encountered Jesus during his freshman year of college. Bill's friend Owen sought to lead him toward Jesus in a tangible way. Owen would meet with him on Monday nights and take him through Scripture.

When Bill led his roommate and a couple other guys to Christ, Owen challenged Bill to disciple two of them on Wednesday nights. Bill was a young believer and didn't think he was ready to take on this task, but he also didn't know any better, so he did it. He went through the exact Scripture on Wednesday nights that Owen led him through on Mondays. Bill just stayed one step ahead (or two days ahead). If the guys brought questions to Bill, he would meet with Owen on Mondays, ask him the questions, and write down the answers.

Bill was developing into a leader. Often in our churches we convey that you have to have deep theological training, years of following Jesus under your belt, and the ability to develop curriculum if you are going to disciple others. You don't have to have all the answers; just stay one step ahead.

I love Bill's story. This discipleship process is how Bill grew so quickly from a skeptic to a disciple and from a disciple into a spiritual leader. While he started to disciple others early in his faith journey, he wasn't abandoned to the task. Owen had given him guardrails to follow. Multiplying our faith into others is not a fast process, but it can begin sooner than we imagine.

Eventually Bill became a pastor, then a church-planting catalyst. He has led many others through a simple discipleship process over the years. I doubt Bill would be the man of God and leader he is today without Owen immediately setting up guardrails and pushing him to reproduce what he was learning.

HOW JESUS DEPLOYED

Perhaps the story you just read about Bill is alarming to you. There is a lie that the North American church has taken hook, line, and sinker. It goes something like this: "We can't set people free to make disciples too soon, or they will teach heresy!"

While all spiritual leaders feel that concern at some level, we must resist giving in to it. What if Bill had been told he needed to go to seminary before he could disciple his roommate? Scripture is clear about not putting people in church leadership positions too quickly, but discipleship is different. Jesus lent us his authority to make disciples. How many people are waiting for authorization to do what Jesus already authorized us to do?

So how did Jesus deploy disciples to make more disciples? Steve Addison describes it like this: "When Jesus' disciples had learned just enough to be dangerous, he sent them out with empty pockets to preach, heal the sick and cast out demons."[7] Jesus never sent out the scribes and Pharisees; they knew too much and obeyed too little. He was looking for fresh and hungry disciples who would be obedient to the call. The book of Acts is crazy and sometimes hilarious, as it chronicles ordinary people being sent out only a step ahead of others while trying to follow the leading of the Holy Spirit.

LEARNERS VERSUS THE LEARNED

We must carefully guard against becoming too educated in mind without our heart, soul, and strength being equally engaged. This is the reason seminary can turn into "cemetery" if learners aren't careful. Neil Cole says, "Christians in the West are educated beyond their obedience."[8] Sometimes we need to put down the book, pick up the phone, and call that person we've been thinking about, or to get out of the church office and get back into discipling relationships.

If we want to keep growing, we must never abandon the posture of practitioner. Lifelong learning has never been more crucial than it is today, in a world that is spinning faster than ever before. Eric Hoffer says, "In a time of drastic change, it is the learners who inherit the future. The learned find themselves equipped to live in a world that no longer exists."[9] People in today's age don't want to learn from those outside the story. "You don't know me" has become the ultimate expression of this reality. If you want to make disciples, you must be actively becoming one. If you want to teach, you must learn like your life depends on it. No one wants to be challenged by those who don't have skin in the game.

DISCIPLESHIP IS VOLUNTARY

People who aren't hungry don't grow. We simply cannot make others grow. This took me years to learn and nearly caused me to burn out in my first few years of ministry. I desired so badly for people to find Jesus and turn their lives around. Eventually I found myself dragging several dead weights around who did not want to grow, and it was sucking the life out of me. Maybe you've felt this before. Maybe you feel like this right now.

It made a huge difference when I started to wait for God to awaken the hunger, and then I would help guide them along. Psalm 127:1-2 is a great warning for us.

Unless the LORD builds the house,
    those who build it labor in vain.
Unless the LORD watches over the city,
    the watchman stays awake in vain.
It is in vain that you rise up early
    and go late to rest,
eating the bread of anxious toil;
    for he gives to his beloved sleep.

We often waste our best energy and effort trying to chase down people for Jesus when they don't even want it. We can catch a vision for their lives that they don't see, so we try to make them see it. It leads to seasons of fruitless busyness. No thanks.

We will fall flat on our faces and live out a gospel-less ministry if we try to do tasks that only God is responsible for. Late nights, early mornings, and anxiety can never replace Jesus as the cornerstone of our ministry. We need to look for hungry people who can benefit from a discipling relationship.

At times I have thought that if I stopped discipling someone, I would be a quitter. I would think, *God doesn't give up on me, so why would I stop meeting with others?* But sometimes we need to stop discipling someone who isn't hungry so we can disciple someone else who is. I'm certainly not saying to stop praying for people and stop sharing Jesus' life-changing gospel with them, but we need to properly steward the limited time and energy God has given us.

A few times I have let leaders on my team know they did not have to continue discipling an apathetic or disinterested person. They later thanked me for freeing them to focus on others. They didn't realize the weight and guilt they were carrying until they were freed to disciple someone else who was hungry.

One of the passages I have always wrestled with is that of the rich young ruler (Luke 18:18-25). Not only does this man of privilege make the wrong decision, but he walks away sad. He was not ready to follow Jesus and sacrifice the last 5 percent of his life. Jesus let him walk away. We must be ready to let people walk away from us if they are not willing to live under the shadow of Jesus. Lowering the bar on discipleship does no one any good. The gospel is always a full commitment.

Occasionally God has acted outside of these parameters in my life. He has asked me to specifically walk with someone who did not seem to have "growth potential." I often wondered whether I was wasting my time, but God would bring me back to this person and show me glimpses of hunger. This holy prodding is always the trump card. The only path to making more disciples is full dependence on God, asking him to help us learn, obey, and emulate the life of Jesus to others.

DISCUSSION QUESTIONS

How are you keeping discipleship at the center of your life?

How are you living as an active learner instead of as the learned?

Which aspect of discipleship is hardest for you: learning, obeying, or reproducing Jesus?

4

THE APPRENTICE

The core competency of any movement is apprenticeship.
DAVE FERGUSON

A long apprenticeship is the most logical way to success. The only alternative is overnight stardom, but I can't give you a formula for that.
CHET ATKINS

Follow me, and I will make you fishers of men.
JESUS

SEVERAL YEARS BACK I wanted to become more consistent in my eating habits. I'm not talking about dieting but eating more consistently in the same restaurant to develop rapport with the staff. The manager slowly warmed up to me and the large groups of leaders who would invade on Friday nights before ministry training. Eventually he and I struck up a friendship, largely built around conversation about our latest woodworking projects. As he invested more free time in woodworking, he started to turn out some really nice projects. Several months later he left the restaurant to escape the great indoors and join a construction team. He reflected just the other day how his carpentry skills have grown exponentially.

For much of the week his hand is on a drill or a saw while learning the tricks of the trade from experienced carpenters. He moved from a casual woodworker to an apprentice.

The word *apprentice* isn't used in many circles today, but it is common in the labor force. Electricians, plumbers, tattoo artists, and hair stylists use it regularly to describe their training process. My tattoo artist, Phil, apprentices people who believe tattooing is part of their destiny. He looks for people who are hungry and have potential, and he takes them under his wing. They flip through tattoo magazines, learn about different styles, hang around other artists, and watch him tattoo clients as he explains his craft. They are thrilled to learn for free.

When they're ready, Phil starts them on a process. They begin by tattooing grapefruits, and then they move on to a hidden portion of their own leg. Then they have to convince a friend to let them practice on them for free. When Phil is confident in their work, they get their own space in the shop.

One day, while I was in Phil's chair (in pain), he gave me his list of what he is looking for in apprentices:

- They fit the relational chemistry of the shop.
- They are willing to work hard, mop the floors, and clean the shop because they want it so badly.
- They would tattoo for free if they had to.

Every apprentice shares this in common: They are hungry for something, and they are willing to work hard to live themselves into it. They are willing to toil, risk, submit, and be stretched in order to walk into their destiny.

This picture of apprenticeship is not too far off from what we should be trying to do as disciples of Jesus, both personally and in our churches. Every human is crafted by God to do good works (Ephesians 2:10). Every human is built with this God-given desire and capacity to come alongside him in Kingdom work.

A CRACK IN THE MODEL

A pastor friend and I were taking an opportunity to reconnect. It was a beautiful day, and we were sitting outside looking up at the mountains outside a local restaurant. It was clear that God had put some holy discontent in my friend. I could tell his soul was spinning like a blender. At the heart of his new conviction was this: His model for leadership development was screwed up. There was a crack in his model.

The paradigm my friend had been following, it turns out, was not what he saw in Scripture. The prevailing leadership paradigm in our world is this: Recruit and hire the most skilled people you can find. It's not bad to look for skilled people and invite them into areas of service, but this can communicate that skill is more important than discipleship. This paradigm often leads to gifted leaders exiting their previous context for a new opportunity in another church or ministry. If the great commission is our paradigm of disciple multiplication, this recruiting process is not even addition—it's subtraction.[1]

Every leader desires significance, and building talented

teams is part of leaving a mark on this world. It's natural to look for those whom God has obviously gifted and put his hand on. We are all drawn to things such as charisma, hipness, talent, and education. But it is important to know your fleshly desires as a leader. Many of the leaders we are trying to recruit are desirable to our ministries only because someone else took the time to disciple and develop them as leaders. Most times it is healthiest to develop leaders from the ground up, from inside the community God has placed you in.

The biblical model for leadership development is this: Train the hungry ones to go and multiply. If we are faithful in praying the Luke 10:2 prayer for God to send us laborers for the harvest, then God will start to turn our eyes away from the talented and toward the hungry. These potential apprentice learners might not look impressive at first, but over time you will be able to see their obedience increase and to watch them bear fruit.

Recently a guy contacted me about what he perceived was a call to plant a church in Colorado. This is a pretty common occurrence, especially after Southerners visit Colorado for their summer vacation and experience the gift of low humidity. He was coming out the next week to look for apartments for his family. I admired his drive to do what God had called him to do and take the next steps. But over the course of phone conversations, his application, his pre-assessment, and a face-to-face interview, it became clear that he was not wired to lead a church plant. He didn't even seem passionate about planting a church. It was clear we could not accept him into the residency. Instead of simply saying no, I affirmed his hunger to learn and assured him that if they still felt the call to Colorado, we would find opportunities in specific ministries under wise leaders who would develop him. I believe church leaders have the responsibility to equip the hungry ones around us.

Believe it or not, baseball players used to come up through the minor leagues and play for one team their whole career. I watched many future major-league stars play in Triple-A, and a few years later I watched those same guys win the World Series. If a team's farm system was not producing the players they needed in two, five, or ten years, then the major-league ball club suffered. We need to get back to this farm-system approach to ministry in our local churches.

THREE REALMS OF APPRENTICESHIP

When it comes to training others, our default setting is to simply provide formal learning opportunities. That is likely how we ourselves were trained. Formal learning is valuable, but apprenticeship is more balanced over the long haul.

Robust apprenticeships include relational, experiential, and formal learning. As I took the risk to move from simply teaching discipleship classes to apprenticing leaders, I found a balanced system that included these three circles. Neither circle is more important than the others, and apprenticeships are healthy only when there is a balance of these three. When anyone approaches me about training others for ministry, I pull out a napkin and draw out these three circles.

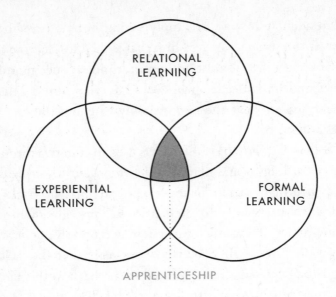

Let's take a look at how Jesus equipped the disciples in these three realms.

Relational learning. The first thing Jesus did with his disciples was to invite them into a relationship. They trusted him enough to follow him. This was common with rabbinical training. Jesus walked alongside people as he equipped them, training the three (Peter, James, and John), the twelve (the apostles), the seventy-two (Luke 10), and the 120 (Acts 1). As the number of people decreased, Jesus' investment of time increased: Whereas the masses would hear him teach and peer at him in crowds or chance encounters, only Peter, James, and John got the backstage pass to his life.

Relational learning is life-on-life and must emphasize challenge and encouragement. In our Frontline Church Planting residency we see great value in having our church planters learn from peers, mentors, and coaches. Ministry coaches guide planters by asking them tough questions and challenging them in new areas. We create roundtable settings for peer learning and encouragement. I call this the "freaks like me club." While it is not as intimate as being in the same room, we launched an online learning and connecting space where planters and future planters can connect from states away and learn from ministry practitioners and from one another.

Apprentices need constant feedback. It's one thing to take a spiritual-gifts assessment, but it's another to have leaders mirror back how they see you live and minister. Gifts are given by God for use in his Kingdom work, but they are confirmed in community. I have seen a lot of fruit from weekly check-ins. People process their leadership challenges and victories with me on a regular basis. Halfway through a residency or apprenticeship, we gather those who have walked alongside our apprentices for a real-life assessment: We share specific areas where we see God working in them, and we acknowledge the specific gifts we have observed through their ministry. We help them build a growth plan for the future. At the end of the apprenticeship, there is a time of affirmation and commissioning. This is similar to the leaders of the early church laying hands on others to affirm their calling and commission them. These are powerful times that frame their ministry forever.

There is power when God's people affirm one another and "pray them into" their next season of ministry. Every follower of Jesus is a missionary, but each path looks unique.

Experiential learning. Studying Jesus' sending process has completely reshaped my view of how "ready" people need to be when they start their ministry. Similar to the story of Owen challenging Bill to disciple the others in his dorm, Jesus sent out the twelve, the seventy-two, and the 120 to experience trial by fire. If we're honest, we would say Jesus sent these groups out before they were "ready." The work they were able to do was not *because* of their training process; it was *part* of their training process. They learned on the go and stumbled into amazing things because of their obedience and the power of God. After returning they debriefed, told victory stories, and headed out on the next mission.

Neil Cole reminds us that we gain mastery of a skill only when it is put into practice and taught to others.[2] Our instincts are to hold on to people until they are overly ready—and nearly lulled to sleep. We must remember when we are "releasing" people that they are still under the authority and guidance of the Holy Spirit.

Few things bug me more than leaders who promise interns spiritual training and then have them simply serve the needs of the leader or church. It's usually a role the church needs but could not afford to pay for. Apprentices, by contrast, are entrusted with meaningful and challenging tasks that are critical to the mission of a church or ministry. Interns make coffee, run copies, and do things we don't have time for, but apprentices jump in the deep end with us. I often say, "This apprenticeship is a safe place to fail. If you aren't failing, I'll be disappointed."

In this respect, an apprenticeship is similar to my kids

learning to walk. They need to fall a lot, but there's still a gate at the top of the stairs. There should be a healthy mix of safety and risk in every apprenticeship. There is no way to manufacture the urgency that comes with experience. (See the appendix for a short assessment of your apprentice culture.)

Formal learning. Some will argue that Jesus trained *only* through life-on-life discipleship. When we look at his ministry, however, we can see that Jesus was very intentionally teaching and instructing. The Sermon on the Mount was truly a sermon. I call it "Jesus' Greatest Hits" because it touches on nearly every major issue humans will face. This was very early in his ministry, and he gave his followers a concentrated formal education. The people sat down, and he proceeded to instruct them on practical areas of life and godliness, giving them a framework for how to live out a practical and poignant gospel. Then Jesus lived out how the rubber would meet the road in these areas during his ministry.

This is why I take people to the Sermon on the Mount directly after teaching them about the Kingdom of God. I am just finishing this up with my daughter. If we are trying to become more like Jesus, then we must start by knowing what Jesus gave his life to. I say to Christians or pre-Christians, "If you like what he's talking about in these three chapters, you're really going to like what he did."

Books and lectures are good sources of formal learning. Make sure to build discussion and relationships into formal-learning times. Have practitioners speak to apprentice learners from the reality of their current experience. Apprentice learners want practical, current, and relevant lessons. Hungry learners value being honest far above being polished.

TEACHERS DON'T CHOOSE WHAT STICKS

We choose what topics we teach apprentices, but we can't choose what they learn. No matter what we think is most impactful, God will drive home the lessons he wants to teach. It's funny how we will try our best to pound home our main point, and people might never forget a side story we briefly mentioned. As I have found in my sermons, my main points aren't usually the main points.

At the end of each apprenticeship or residency, I ask people to share their biggest takeaways. It used to surprise me, but almost without fail these have been the top five.

Sabbath. People share how they stumbled through victories and failure of engaging or avoiding Sabbath. This is experiential learning.

Conflict resolution. People faced normal life conflict from their proximity to others, and they were forced to resolve the conflict. This is both relational and experiential.

Time management. Through experiencing stress and eliminating it through crucial planning, every apprentice I've ever had has gained ground in this area. It takes work to manage time well, and it certainly takes work to help others learn this. This is relational and experiential.

Family life. Past apprentices got to see me in the madness of having kids. One group even got to support our family as we traveled to Ethiopia to bring our adopted kids home. What they observed during adoption was much more intense than any season on ministry I've faced in the church. They got a front-row seat to watch my wife and me journey through our own relational and experiential learning.

The SHARRP principles. The remainder of this book will walk through six movement principles that have emerged as the core of our apprentice training: Healthy discipleship is simple, holistic, adaptable, regular, reproducible, and positive. Training in these movement principles is formal and experiential. It's been significant for our apprentices.

Only one of these takeaways—the SHARRP principles—emphasizes formal learning. They aren't the only formal training we offer, but relational and experiential learning have proven to be stickier than most of our formal learning experiences. Ironically, relationship and experience are the realms of training most often absent from ministry. John Maxwell famously said, "We teach what we know, but we reproduce what we are."[3] While teaching what we know is important, reproducing Jesus into the lives of others is crucial.

JESUS AND THE APPRENTICE MODEL

Jewish culture in Jesus' day trained apprentices. In fact, Jesus most likely learned carpentry through apprenticeship. He held tools, did the dirty work, and eventually got to try it out. At some point he was set free as a carpenter.

Jesus apprenticed the disciples. English missionary Roland Allen points out the differences between how Jesus apprenticed leaders and how we usually train leaders:

Christ trained His leaders by taking them with
Him as He went about teaching and healing,
doing the work which they, as missionaries,
would do; we train in institutions. He trained
a very few with whom He was in the closest
personal relation; we train many who simply
pass through our schools with a view to an
examination and an appointment.[4]

We never graduate from Jesus' apprenticeship. In fact,
the more we learn the life of Jesus, obey his commands, and
multiply him into others, the less self-confident we feel. This
is the upside-down nature of the Kingdom at work: When he
becomes more, the only natural reaction is for us to become
less. Look at the life of Paul. The more he obeyed God and
saw fruit, the less worthy he felt to minister.

In our life on mission with Jesus, we are called to be "player
coaches." People will apprentice under us at times, but we all
are apprenticing under Jesus. We are not "qualified" because
of a degree, ministry experience, or fruitful growth; we are
qualified because Jesus is the author and perfecter of our
story. God has created good works for us to do, and he has
them waiting for us. He is the gracious Master, and we are
merely servants who get to carry out the work.

I have known Zach since he came to know Jesus in early
high school. We have done a lot of life together and have
had a lot of deep conversations. Zach was my apprentice
for a few years. He is winsome and talented, and God has
crafted Zach's story to reach a lot of people. He was a gifted

guy, he had been developed and equipped, and he was more ready than he realized. At a certain point I sensed that if I didn't push Zach out of the nest a bit, I would actually hold him back from having a greater Kingdom impact. He began leading two groups and grew by leaps and bounds in his discipleship capacity. While it was hard for me to take this step with Zach, it removed me as a barrier in his ministry.

Jesus has already commissioned his people. At times we will need to challenge and recommission those we are equipping, as we remind them they have already been given authority to do great things in the name of Jesus. At times we will need to decommission ourselves in order to give them the freedom to do what Jesus has authorized them to do.

We must be living out the message we are passing on to others. Our leadership must reflect our own apprenticeship. Alan Hirsch writes,

> Instead of adopting the aloof, hierarchical, top-down approach to leadership, we should, like the biblical leaders (Moses, David, Jesus, Paul), *lead from the front and not from the rear*. . . . The teacher must also be a practitioner. We must all have a hand in, and a direct stake in, the ideas we are proclaiming—we must be personally risking and experiencing what we are calling others to do. Our capacity to be inspirational leaders, not simply transactional ones, hinges on this.[5]

DISCUSSION QUESTIONS

Which of the three realms of apprenticeship—relational, experiential, formal—is currently your strongest? Your weakest?

How do you need to grow in developing an apprentice culture?

What aspects of apprenticeship are hardest for you to embrace? Why?

PART TWO
PRINCIPLES

5

DISCIPLESHIP MUST BE SIMPLE

If a person can't remember and immediately implement something after one meeting, it's too complex.
JON TYSON

Simple can be harder than complex. You have to work hard to get your thinking clean to make it simple. But it's worth it in the end, because once you get there, you can move mountains.
STEVE JOBS

It is a simple task to make things complex, but a complex task to make them simple.
MEYER'S LAW

FEW WORDS STRIKE FEAR in me like these: ". . . lest the cross of Christ be emptied of its power." In 1 Corinthians 1:17-18, the apostle Paul confronts the tendency to complexify the gospel.

> Christ did not send me to baptize but to preach the gospel, and not with words of eloquent wisdom, lest the cross of Christ be emptied of its power.
> For the word of the cross is folly to those who are perishing, but to us who are being saved it is the power of God.

We can be so wrapped up in big words and complicated tasks that our efforts literally become devoid of God's power. As long as we think we are impressive and prolific, people won't see that Jesus is. We take the simple message of the gospel and jack it up. We accidentally add insulating layers and cool off the boiling-hot message that Jesus died to get us off death row.

Sometimes the greatest barrier to seeing gospel fruit in our ministry is ourselves. If the Cross is not at the center of our ministry, we have gotten the whole thing wrong.

The more educated we get, the more we have to guard against losing the simplicity of the Good News. Father Herbert Kelly challenges us to "take care that our trained men do not lose in simplicity and directness of character what they gain in intellectual development."[1] It's as if the potency of the gospel gets diluted rather than enhanced, like a spoonful of lemonade in a bathtub.

Simplicity should be a virtue of the Christian life and a virtue for ministry. Simplicity yields both clarity and power. A few years ago, my family went to the mountains for a family reunion. One night I was walking away from the bonfire with my three-year-old son. He saw a big cross and turned to me. "Daddy," he said, "that is a cross. Jesus died on it to save you, me, Mommy, and anyone else from their sins." I was amazed at the clarity of the sermon he had just given me. That's what it's all about, but we so easily forget it.

THE PROBLEM OF COMPLEXITY

I had the privilege of watching God do some simplifying work in an apprentice of mine. David was discipling middle school students and leading a team of leaders when he was reminded of the simplicity of the great commission: "Go . . . and make disciples of all nations, baptizing them in the name of the Father and of the Son and of the Holy Spirit, teaching them to observe all that I have commanded you" (Matthew 28:19-20). "Too often," David says, "we translate it, 'Go make complicated systems of discipleship that involve three different video segments for four different time slots in your small group that meets on the first and third Monday and Thursday except on the even-numbered months.'" David felt God telling him to make several changes in the ministry, although he knew it wouldn't be received very well. He dialed into simplicity that pushed him toward gospel clarity, and I have watched his influence explode. In his current role, David is living out the call to "make disciples who make disciples."

It really needs to be that simple. We tend to make discipleship so complicated, and as a result of this, we get burned out or frustrated because we're not seeing results. And if we don't get burned out as the disciplers, then the people we are "discipling" will probably get confused by how complicated we made it.

A lot is at stake here. If we make discipleship too complicated, people won't understand how they could possibly do the same thing with others.

Think back to your roster of high school teachers. Chances are, the ones you learned the most from took complex topics and delivered them in simple ways. I still remember the diagrams Mr. Butler drew in physics class and the grammar rules from Ms. Degaynor's English class. Some teachers, on the other hand, were another kind of brilliant: They had a lot going on in their brains, but they had no idea how to simplify it so others could understand.

Complexity limits the distance an idea can travel. Remember the game "Telephone" from when you were little? Things that are too complex will get left behind or lost in translation along the way. In their book *On the Verge,* Dave Ferguson and Alan Hirsch see simplicity as a key to the future of the church.

> If the message is complex, it will not be easily
> remembered, understood, lived out, or transferred
> from person to person. But if the message is powerful
> and simple, it will be easily remembered, understood,
> lived out, and passed with viral mobility from one
> generation of [Christ] followers to the next.[2]

Simplicity is the key to any discipleship process. Mike Breen refers to this need for simplicity as staying "lightweight and low maintenance."[3] Most churches I have spent time with, by contrast, have discipleship processes that are heavy and high maintenance. Many pastors and ministry leaders I meet are tired and bogged down with secondary concerns on the periphery of the church. Committee meetings, building concerns, and trying to keep a few folks in the church happy can take a lot out of you. Not only does it create a heaviness of structure that can wear you down, but it also can create spiritual heaviness that can exhaust your soul.

Sometimes ego creates the heaviness. Sometimes preserving legacy events of the church creates the heaviness. Sometimes it's purely overprogramming and overscheduling that leaves ministry leaders feeling weighed down. But everyone can find a few ways to simplify. I dare you.

TESTING SIMPLICITY

I spend a lot of my time equipping leaders for ministry in different environments. Those I lead will tell you I love diagrams. I've never seen a meeting that couldn't get better with a few boxes or circles. My simplicity test is whether the concept, principle, or idea in question can effectively be passed on to others using just a napkin. Some of the best things I've ever learned were written on napkins at restaurants.

Diagrams are important to how we learn and even more important to how concepts are passed on to others. If your processes for making disciples can't be taught and applied quickly and effectively, then you should question your method.

Like the napkin test, repeated pithy phrases or mantras can get stuck in the lives of your leaders and become a part of your culture. Lacing conversations and teaching with simplicity can solidify culture and reinforce core values.

Dan was highly impacted during his apprenticeship by our focus on simplicity. "It is hard to lead a small group," he told us, "in which you must study and prepare for hours each week before the meeting. Complicated group systems do not encourage long-lasting small groups." Dan helped to shift the ministry he leads by simplifying the small-group structure. He implemented a single set of simple questions that empowered the learners to study Scripture. This shifted the groups from a teacher-centric curriculum based on the leader's knowledge to a learning focus on Scripture. Dan is helping to leave a legacy in his ministry by letting people experience for themselves the simplicity of the gospel as they engage the Bible.

The simplicity principle could literally save the life and future of your ministry. We all want to leave a gospel legacy. Just make sure your method is simple enough that it sticks.

DISCUSSION QUESTIONS

When have you accidentally emptied the Cross of its power through complexity?

What would it take to be able to pass on your process of multiplying disciples using a napkin?

What is the simplest means possible to equip the leaders around you for ministry?

6

DISCIPLESHIP MUST BE HOLISTIC

Knowing the heart of Jesus and loving him are the same thing.
HENRI NOUWEN

Without the Way, there is no going; without the Truth, there is no knowing; without the Life, there is no living.
THOMAS À KEMPIS

Those who aren't following Jesus aren't his followers. It's that simple.
SCOT MCKNIGHT

IMAGINE YOU ARE COUNTING DOWN the days to your wedding. Somewhere between the flower order and figuring out the assigned seating for the reception, you start to get cold feet. The commitment is just too much. Instead of breaking the engagement, you elect another option: narrow down the vows and give away less of yourself.

As you write your own vows, you make sure you clearly state that your weekends will always be your own. You will get to make all vacation plans. You won't be spending even one night with the in-laws. You'll never share a checking account.

Good luck with that marriage.

This sounds a lot like what we do with God. We offer pieces of ourselves but hold back the things that really matter to us.

We have glazed over much of the Old Testament today, especially when we talk about loving God. But when Jesus sums up the nature of discipleship in Matthew 22:34-40, he points directly to the Old Testament:

> Hear, O Israel: The LORD our God, the LORD is one. You shall love the LORD your God with all your heart and with all your soul and with all your might. And these words that I command you today shall be on your heart. You shall teach them diligently to your children, and shall talk of them when you sit in your house, and when you walk by the way, and when you lie down, and when you rise. You shall bind them as a sign on your hand, and they shall be as frontlets between your eyes. You shall write them on the doorposts of your house and on your gates.
>
> DEUTERONOMY 6:4-9

Unless we have a complete view of God and ourselves, we will have a skewed view of what it means to be a disciple.

I have always found this passage intriguing, known among the Jews as the *Shema*. Let's take a look at several areas the Shema instructs us about.

God and man. First, this Scripture turned a polytheistic culture on its head, saying there is only one true God. In similar fashion, it shifts our view of us from just one person to a multifaceted being: heart, soul, and might. (Jesus adds the mind to this list.) There is only one God, but humans have many pieces, and all must point to him.

Space and time. Next we see that every space in life is sacred. Sitting in the house, walking down the road, lying down at night, waking up in the morning, and everything in between—all are sacred spaces. The expectation is clear that spiritual truths are being intentionally passed down to the next generation in all of these spaces.

Word and deed. It's clear that our devotion needs to encompass both word and deed. If something is present on your hand, you will see it in everything you do; and if something sits right between your eyes, it is present in everything you look at. I will never forget seeing Orthodox Jews in old-city Jerusalem wearing these little black boxes called phylacteries tied to their heads. The combination of eyes and hands would make you doubly aware that you are marked by God before you sin or before you bless.

Inside and outside. Your gates separate your home from the outside world and bring protection. Your doorposts signal the beginning of your home. The spiritual life should be lived equally in private and in public, in your home and out in the streets. I believe the home is the most underused ministry space. Instead of being refuges from ministry, our homes should be hubs for God's grace to spill into our neighborhoods.

As the Shema demonstrates, everything is spiritual territory: our whole identity, all spaces of our lives, all of our actions in private and in public. Discipleship is a full-time gig. Alan and Debra Hirsch say,

> The clear implication is that nothing in life,
> culture, and the human experience lies outside of

> this all-encompassing claim. No false dualisms,
> no sacred-secular splits—all of our lives, including
> our sexuality, work, play, home, politics, and
> economics, can, and indeed must, become
> aspects of our worship to the One True God.[1]

Let's make no mistake about it: God wants it all.

4-D DISCIPLESHIP

Before we ever gave anything to God, he gave us an identity. Even Jesus was identified as the Son in whom God was well pleased at baptism, *before* his formal ministry began (Matthew 3:17). Our identity in Christ comes before the work we do, not because of the work we do.

When we realize our identity as God's children, it should change everything about the way we live and minister. On their best and worst days at school, whether they were honored on a stage or whether they spent the afternoon in the principal's office, I still love my kids. They are my kids, and I love them.

Meetings, teaching, play, meals, paychecks, training, schedules, parenting, vacations, Sabbath, learning, and eating must all be surrendered to God—heart, soul, mind, and strength. I call this Shema-centered approach "4-D discipleship." I apply heart, soul, mind, and strength in the following ways.

- *Heart:* our passion and will. What are you creating or striving after?

- *Soul:* our connection with the eternal; our spiritual imagination. What are the God-inspired dreams you are thinking about and praying for?
- *Mind:* our pursuit of knowledge and depth. What are you hungry to learn about and investigate?
- *Strength:* our rhythms of expending time, energy, and talent. What do you spend time and energy on in your life?

These four aspects of our identity were how Jesus characterized the Shema when asked. But then he went on. "The second [command] is this: 'You shall love your neighbor as yourself.' There is no other commandment greater than these" (Mark 12:31). Jesus connects loving others with loving God, yet he still communicates that loving God is where it all starts.

The order of these verses has changed how I seek to love others. I often catch myself trying to love others from my own strength, even starting to get cynical as I do. When we try to generate love for others on our own, we get to the end of ourselves pretty quickly. If we aren't connected to God as we minister, we will only grow to the size and capacity of ourselves. We've all had seasons where we tried to love others from our own desire. There is simply not enough desire in us as we seek to love those at work, our spouse, our physical neighbors, our children, and our friends. If we aren't guided by God's love, we're sunk.

If we follow the proper order of loving God first and then loving others, we will have to relearn how we minister. Ministry is the overflow of our hearts. Sometimes we are trying to hold back a flood from the Father, and sometimes we are trying to tap a dry well. I believe that the number-one reason for burnout in pastors stems from trying to give something that they don't have themselves. The danger comes when we keep leading out of that place of emptiness because we believe our reputation, relationships, or finances depend on it. This is a scary place to get stuck.

EVERYTHING IS CONNECTED

I have a friend who recently celebrated four years of sobriety. You can't tell him that his addiction is just one isolated area of his life. His whole life was turned upside down by alcohol and drugs, and his recovery touches on all aspects of his life today. Everything in us is connected.

I refer to college students as "the most unbalanced people on the planet." College life is not built for health. There is a massive swing from cramming for exams to having virtually no responsibilities over breaks, from staying up all night eating donuts and Ramen noodles to napping the afternoon away, from no space to get alone in a dorm to total isolation at times. College life can be a deeply unhealthy season of life. I remember getting excited to go home for Christmas break. Stressed and exhausted from procrastinating on papers until 1:00 a.m., I couldn't wait for the break to begin. I envisioned myself spending more time in God's Word and thanking him for the glory of Sabbath.

Despite having lots of expendable time, I stepped out of my busy routine and got even more unhealthy! Sleeping in late turned into forgoing exercise, which led to eating poorly, which led to watching too much television. Suddenly it was time to head back to school, and I had somehow avoided listening to the voice of God for several weeks. When one area of life suffers, others will suffer.

Our lives ebb and flow based on all of who we are, not just one part. We all have had very healthy seasons of life and seasons that were downright unhealthy. When we start to eat poorly, sleep less, work too much or too little, or struggle with sin, all parts of us suffer. It is not long before we are turning the music up in our car so we don't have to hear God's whispers, and we haven't picked up our Bible in a while. Anyone who says they can live without discipline in one of these areas is heading toward a crash in all areas.

Attending to only one aspect of a person is how "performance-ism" takes root. We find ourselves hiding behind a false self, pretending. We seek to cover the cracks and inconsistencies in our lives by limiting the scope of our discipleship, elevating where we are strong and minimizing where we are weak. We become modern-day Pharisees, touting our pious deeds all over social media.

It's amazing to me what we will pray for or "hold people accountable for" and what we won't touch with a ten-foot pole. We won't hesitate to pray for a home loan to come through on an expensive car or a home we can't afford. Yet things like anger, eating habits, marital issues, debt, chasing the American Dream, budgets, sex, prayer, technology addiction, and over-working are taboo. Many of our discipleship boundaries have more to do with America than they do with Abba.

When we take 4-D discipleship seriously, with a careful

focus on heart, soul, mind, and strength, we risk people leaving our groups or churches to find "safer" ones where they can avoid dealing with uncomfortable areas. A pastor friend of mine has been vulnerable before his staff and his congregation about his issues with anger. He has felt an amazing freedom to "struggle well" with God in his community. That has allowed others to drop pretense and share what they are actually struggling with. As we commit to 4-D discipleship, spiritual strongholds can be acknowledged and broken— even in areas we had no idea we were struggling in.

Every discipleship relationship or group must focus on the heart, soul, mind, and strength if we hope to find alignment with the life of Christ. Are you willing to invite Christ to shape every area of your life? Are you willing to go "out of spiritual bounds" to delve into new areas of discipleship with those you disciple?

DISCUSSION QUESTIONS

How do your discipleship processes need to expand to attend to the heart, soul, mind, and strength?

In which area of your life are you most tempted to put on a false front?

Into what taboo areas of your life do you need to invite the Spirit and others?

7

DISCIPLESHIP MUST BE
ADAPTABLE

The most effective movements are prepared to change everything about themselves except their basic beliefs.
STEVE ADDISON

We must play down our longing for certainty, accept what is risky, and live by improvisation and experiment.
HANS KÜNG

Things are happening so fast and communities are changing so much that even the model you design today will have to be redesigned and reengineered tomorrow.
BOB ROBERTS JR.

I SPENT MOST of my childhood outdoors. As a kid I was always building forts and playing with fire. (I have more than a few fire stories, but I will save those for another day.) During high school summers I worked all week and preferred to spend weekends fishing in the river, wearing ragged jean shorts (aka "jorts") and no shirt. During one college semester I received college credit to spend three months paddling rivers, backpacking through forests, rapelling into canyons, and camping in snowfields, all the while learning to survive and lead people.

Thousands of hours in the woods paved the way for those three months of cooking, tending to sick comrades, repairing gear, setting up tents, and navigating near-emergencies. Over time we gained confidence that we could apply the few principles we had learned in nearly any situation. It was never pretty, but we traveled a lot of miles, overcame a lot of obstacles, and "MacGyvered" our way home safely from every adventure.

I grew up on *MacGyver*, the TV show about a man with a mullet who could make bombs with paper clips and baking soda. He always found himself in dire situations, and he always had a solution. Some kids wanted to be Batman; I wanted to be MacGyver.

We could take a few lessons from the man with the mullet. We need to leave the confines of safe church behind and become more comfortable with "MacGyvering." Things look nice and neat in the latest book or at the latest conference— until we actually begin. We make great plans for ministry, but then our ministry leads us into the wilderness of the lives around us. Things start getting messy, and we have to adapt in real time to the real lives of real people.

In *The Forgotten Ways*, Alan Hirsch compares the reproducibility of the early church to the systems of al-Qaeda. Both, he observes, are network systems. The whole organism is reproducible from one single cell, which carries the complete DNA, ethos, and message of the whole. Communities with this much internal consistency are simple and highly adaptable expressions of Jesus' church. Living rooms, coffeehouses, parks, pubs, and schools become sanctuaries for

DISCIPLESHIP MUST BE ADAPTABLE

gospel application and faithful presence. The leaders of these communities need not carry the weight of a heavy church structure. They can exist as one small appendage of a larger church body. The effectiveness of these communities of missionaries rests in their *flexibility.*

One of the greatest joys I find in working with church planters is that they are some of the most flexible people on the planet. They have to be. We live in a dynamic, ever-changing world. Carriers of a message must remain flexible to tailor it to the complexities of changing environments. Context determines the methods. When we take the church out of the building, things get messy, and we lose any control we thought we had.

ACTS 2: THE CHURCH OF THE BOTH/AND

The second chapter of Acts is widely used to make a case for the house-church model. But if we look closely, it is much more than that.

> And they devoted themselves to the apostles' teaching and the fellowship, to the breaking of bread and the prayers. And awe came upon every soul, and many wonders and signs were being done through the apostles. And all who believed were together and had all things in common. And they were selling their possessions and belongings and distributing the proceeds to all, as any had need. And day by day, attending the temple together and breaking bread in their homes, they received their food with glad and

generous hearts, praising God and having favor with
all the people. And the Lord added to their number
day by day those who were being saved.

ACTS 2:42-47

While we could write volumes on these six verses, I want to
focus on the balance of their gatherings in three particular
ways.

Temple and home. The Acts 2 church gathered in homes.
They also continued to worship at the temple. When it came
to private and public space, for the Acts 2 church it wasn't
either/or; it was both/and. They gathered in homes, scattered
for daily life, and gathered again in the temple.

Ritual and freshness. Worshiping at the temple meant con-
tinuing the age-old rituals and tradition of temple life. But
they simultaneously experienced the freshness of the apostles'
teaching, new generosity, communion meals, and great signs
and wonders.

Doing and being. The early Christians had healthy
rhythms of "doing" church while also "being" the church.
The power of the Holy Spirit fell on these people, and new
fruit overflowed.

It's tempting to focus on the half of each of these pairs
that we feel most comfortable with. When we do, our focus
swings like a pendulum from one paradigm to the next.
Many shifts in the church's history can be attributed to this
kind of pendulum swing: Neglect in one season results in
zealous overcompensation in the next. We would be wise to
learn from the many both/ands of the church in Acts 2.

DIVINE CRISIS

Whenever I am visiting other cities, people ask me about Colorado Springs. They want to know what it's like in the so-called evangelical mecca. They are intrigued to hear about the spiritual temperature, the realities of the city, and the unique challenges to the gospel here. I assure you it's a tale of two cities.

Every city faces unique roadblocks to the gospel; in Colorado Springs our biggest roadblock is the perceived stability of Christendom. It is, indeed, a beautiful city at the base of Pikes Peak that seems safe for raising a family, enjoying the mountains, getting involved in a church, seeking economic prosperity, and even being involved with world-influencing ministries. But the reality is that church attendance is on par with or lower than the national average, and many people in our city are very resistant to the gospel and involvement in the church. It is a very polarized city.

Meanwhile, in a relatively short season my city experienced two devastating fires and two floods. Some spaces that were picturesque now look postapocalyptic. Homes were ruined and families displaced, and the equilibrium of our city was rocked. Some were able to rebuild, but some lost everything they had. We grieved with families through the loss of homes and dreams, but we also experienced the church like never before. These divine crises brought our city together and showed an amazing picture of the church. Christians truly became lights in our city.

There were a few weeks when the whole city nearly shut down and turned its attention to caring for our people. As we pushed regular tasks aside, several folks asked me, "When are we going to get back to business as usual at the church?" My response was, "This is business as usual!" Churches were still digging into disaster-relief efforts to serve the community a year or more after these catastrophes. Disaster-relief teams came to clear property, help families search for valuables, and pray with families. Churches close to burn areas said they had never felt so connected to the community and had never experienced that kind of spiritual curiosity in their parishes.

Eventually our eyes lifted from the evening news, but the seeds planted during these times continue to bear fruit. We must not manufacture crises, but we must stand ready to adapt to how God wants to use his church, whatever the circumstance. David Bosch rightly says, "To encounter crisis is to encounter the possibility of truly being the *church*."[1] The church is designed to merge into unity during crisis.

MISSIONARIES AND ADAPTABILITY

The word *missionary* is synonymous with adaptability. By nature a missionary steps into someone else's history, rhythms, culture, schedule, plans, economy, diet, and language. The journey into missionary life finds us giving up our rights, releasing any past privilege we were gripping on to, and learning to live as exiles. This is often more of a ripping free than a willing submission. But however it happens, dying to our old preferences shows respect for the new culture and an openness to learn in order to partner in the mission of God.

We all are missionaries. We are simultaneously seeking to make sense of the world we live in while proclaiming and embodying the gospel. Saint Patrick was known for adapting his methods to meet his context. He willingly returned to Ireland to flesh out the gospel among the very hostile tribes who had enslaved him. He befriended those who had mistreated him and those whom the "civilized" world considered savages. The way Patrick served the Irish was unprecedented. Steve Addison explains it this way:

> In contrast to the static, rigid and anchored nature of the Roman church, Celtic monasticism was supremely adaptable, flexible and transferable. While the heart of the gospel remained the same, Patrick communicated the gospel in ways that affirmed the best of Celtic culture, ensuring that the Irish could follow Christ without having to become Romans. The forms changed to fit the context and to serve the needs of an expanding movement while the unchanging gospel remained at the center of the movement.[2]

We can take many lessons from the adaptable methods of Saint Patrick. We feel like aliens in our own culture some days, but as missionaries we must choose to give up the illusion of control if we are to see a great gospel harvest.

SHIFT HAPPENS

When we have powerful experiences in churches, small groups, or discipleship groups, we can become convinced that *this* is the way discipleship should be done. It can be tempting to think, *I finally found the perfect recipe for discipleship that has been hiding this whole time!* But there is no step-by-step instruction manual for making disciples.

The wide breadth of churches is always encouraging to me. I love getting to experience vastly different forms of church, from the biker church, to the traditional church that exclusively sings hymns, to the new church meeting in a living room, to the church that meets in a park picnic shelter. Just as church forms are unique, discipleship in every context should also be unique. Every discipler must be a student of his or her context.

A friend of mine named Steve described a major shift from reliance on a model to reliance on the Spirit. Steve led a group of hyperactive students. It was like herding cats. He tried to implement the exact process he had learned from his men's group. Let's just say that plane didn't fly. Gradually he came to understand where the guys in his group were developmentally, spiritually, socially, and emotionally. He adapted his approach to better fit the guys, and he saw more development in their discipleship. The goal of both groups, the men and the students, was the same. But the implementation of the goal had to shift. We must be students of our context if we hope to reach people within it.

GOD'S GRACE AND OUR OBEDIENCE

Every time I read through the book of Acts, I am fascinated. How did the church expand so rapidly? Sociologist Rodney Stark was fascinated enough to spend several years and a whole book, *The Rise of Christianity*, answering this question: "How did a tiny and obscure messianic movement from the edge of the Roman Empire dislodge classical paganism and become the dominant faith of Western civilization?"[3] It is a fascinating book.

We often try to turn the movement we observe in the book of Acts into a model. But what caused the explosive growth in the early church wasn't their model but their dedication to follow God at all costs and adapt to the movement of the Holy Spirit. The church grew by the grace of God and through the obedience of people to share the gospel narrative. The church grew with very little structure, but it also grew with the addition of structure. It grew in times of persecution, but it also grew in times of peace. It grew in town squares, but it also grew in homes.

What model should we adopt from the early church? It is impossible to manufacture a single model based on the early church; it was far too adaptive. These early Christians invited the Holy Spirit to take hold of them as they lived ordinary lives with extraordinary love.

Each fall, Frontline Church Planting hosts the annual Multiply Conference. Each year we try to take a different risk with the conference. Throughout the course of the year I meet with a lot of people, and I try to put my ear to the ground and ask, "What is the Spirit speaking to gospel leaders in Colorado?" These become the things we try to address at the conference. One year, as we reflected on what God seemed to be collectively speaking to the church in Colorado, the phrase "uncomfortable shift" came to mind. Leaders seemed to be experiencing significant detours in their ministry. Heading into the conference, we decided to open the conference with something called "The Paradigm Sessions." Each speaker would have five minutes on the main stage to share their biggest paradigm shift in the last five years, and how God had shaped their story through it. Five years in five minutes: This was either an amazing idea or a terrible one.

There was great anticipation as we kicked off that year's conference with "The Paradigm Sessions." Fifteen local leaders shared how they had shifted their lives and ministries as God had told them to. It was an incredibly powerful time! What we noticed afterward was that every session included a story of the Holy Spirit guiding someone, through a shout or a nudge. It was inspiring to hear the obedience and humility of everyone who shared that day. We are now a few years into "The Paradigm Sessions," and for some, this is the most impactful time during the whole conference.

As we pursue structure for sustaining our disciple-making ministry, we must remain open to what the Spirit speaks to us and be obedient to respond. I continue to ask two questions I borrowed from Mike Breen: "What is God speaking to you?" and "What are you gonna do about it?" There is such variety in the answers to these questions.

When you practice listening to God and responding, two key things happen.

It brings fresh life. It always amazes me how God speaks to each person differently about specific areas of their lives when we are open to hear him. There is always variance in what people hear God speaking to them as they read the Bible. Group times stay fresh as templates give way to the movement of God's Spirit.

It keeps us accountable to God, not one another. Often, accountability groups fail because one person applies his or her own struggles to other members of the group. In the human sense this falls short, because neither the person making the challenge nor the person being challenged takes ownership. A human being is inserting his or her voice where God's voice should be. When we hold others accountable to what God speaks to them, by contrast, we all are pursuing direct obedience to God and supporting one another in that quest.

I mentioned Zach earlier. It has been amazing to watch God minister so personally to Zach over the years. He has lived out a Spirit-led ministry discipling tattoo artists, bartenders, athletes, and students—young and old alike. He couldn't lead the bartender in the same way he led the college student, so he adapted his ministry accordingly. Today he spends time leading and equipping different groups in different ways. Visiting Zach was one of the highlights of a summer trip: We prayer-walked the city he ministers in, and I watched him dream about different ways to bring the gospel to that context.

As ministers of the gospel, we need to ask God for wisdom and discernment in how we can lead and disciple the unique and diverse body of Christ. Just as Jesus and his disciples spread the best news in the world in unique and intentional ways, we have to be adaptable in the way we are teaching others to walk in the way of Jesus.

The Spirit literally delivers God's truth to us. There are many different viewpoints on the Holy Spirit: Some take liberties around the work of the Holy Spirit that make me uncomfortable. Others come from traditions where the Holy Spirit is the weird uncle no one ever talks about. However nuanced your view of the Spirit might be, the Holy Spirit leads us toward faithful gospel proclamation:

> When the Spirit of truth comes, he will guide you
> into all the truth, for he will not speak on his own
> authority, but whatever he hears he will speak, and
> he will declare to you the things that are to come.
> He will glorify me, for he will take what is mine
> and declare it to you.
>
> JOHN 16:13-14

The Holy Spirit comes with God's authority, so listening to the Spirit will always force us to adapt our ways to the will of God.

Form, strategy, and methods are ever-changing. The ministry principles of Jesus, however, don't change. I'm all for innovation, creativity, and new models of church, but it becomes dangerous when we rely on new models instead of timeless guardrails. Our world is changing at a rapid rate, and what works today has no guarantee of working tomorrow. We are adaptable as a matter of principle. Spiritual leaders who leave a legacy will be the ones whose methods are guided by timeless principles.

Do you trust the leading of the Holy Spirit? We have only two choices: to trust what the Spirit is asking us to do or to resist, to submit to the Holy Spirit or to grieve the Holy

Spirit. I have had many times when I didn't know whether God had spoken to me or whether it was just my crazy idea. Every spiritual leader will face this tension. I have heard God wrongly before and felt like a fool. Maybe you have too. That's just part of life in Christ. One of the most vulnerable things we can do is follow the Spirit of truth when we don't know what the results will be. Adapting our methods will require faith.

If you set disciple-making as your true north—your guiding principle of ministry—and you rely on the power and leading of the Holy Spirit to inform your methods, your ministry can change entire communities. The potential is limitless. The church needs big doses of adaptability as we seek to make disciples in an increasingly diverse and complex world. The early church did it; I'm crazy enough to believe we can too.

DISCUSSION QUESTIONS

How are you personally and your church collectively living out the both/ands of the Acts 2 church?

What timeless principles do you cling to in your ministry?

How have you experienced the church coming alive in a time of crisis?

8

DISCIPLESHIP MUST BE REGULAR

Part of courage is simple consistency.
PEGGY NOONAN

No movement can be sustained on crisis experiences alone. Spiritual disciplines prepare the way for, and support, life-changing experiences. All the great movement pioneers learned both to surrender to God in crisis and to seek his grace through the practice of spiritual disciplines.
STEVE ADDISON

When you run the marathon, you run against the distance, not against the other runners and not against the time.
HAILE GEBRSELASSIE, WORLD CHAMPION MARATHONER

THREE OF US SAT WAITING at a table in a restaurant on the edge of a small Montana town. I was nervous to spend a few days with someone who has accidentally mentored me. Eugene Peterson, whom some have called "the bishop of today's church," has had a massive impact on many people, especially pastors. Hundreds of his pithy sayings have pierced the exoskeleton of my ministry and hit me at heart level. I knew the general flow of his story from his memoir, *The Pastor.* I have seen Scripture afresh in his paraphrase, *The Message.* The Lord used the next few days to fill me. He and Jan were as delightful and honest as I had hoped for.

After good food, serious conversation, and a lot of laughs, one of the other pastors asked the zinger: "So, what is your biggest piece of advice for young pastors like us?"

Eugene pondered for a minute. Then, in his low, soft voice, he said, "Stay as long as you possibly can, even when times get dark."

Looking back on those three days and the resounding message of Eugene's writings, I hear a recurring theme: *consistency*. The importance of consistency in ministry has never stoked my passion, but I have come to understand how crucial regularity is. There is no replacement for the longevity of a person who keeps showing up. Discipleship—what Eugene calls "a long obedience in the same direction"—is not a dash but a steady journey.

My family is seeking to "make a scene for Jesus" in our neighborhood and city. People are skeptical of things that come and go quickly, of flash-in-the-pan relationships. When we began to put our roots in our neighborhood and sought to embody Jesus there, we knew the most important thing we could do was to just keep showing up. Consistency yields credibility. We have not done anything glitzy or impressive, but we have gained favor with the administration at the local elementary school, long-time residents of the neighborhood, and elementary school parents—largely because we have just kept showing up. God does the rest, and he does it well.

Much of life is lived in the mundane between the valley and the peak. Making disciples is not glorious. Many days it feels as if those whom I invest in are sliding backwards like a two-wheel-drive car on an icy hill. We all have to fight the temptation to seek greener grass or shinier ministry opportunities. Making disciples requires us to engage God in the regular, ordinary, and even mundane areas of life as we pursue faithfulness to the great commission and the great commissioner. Making disciples requires us to shed any desire to be rock-star leaders on big stages, and instead seek faithfulness to apply ourselves to loving God and loving others. Disciple-makers are very ordinary people who take God's mission seriously.

SEEDS AND REGULARITY

We've all heard the parable of the sower (Matthew 13:3-8), but it has a lot to speak to us today. It describes four types of seeds.

> A sower went out to sow. And as he sowed, some
> seeds fell along the path, and the birds came and
> devoured them. Other seeds fell on rocky ground,
> where they did not have much soil, and immediately
> they sprang up, since they had no depth of soil,
> but when the sun rose they were scorched. And
> since they had no root, they withered away. Other
> seeds fell among thorns, and the thorns grew up
> and choked them. Other seeds fell on good soil
> and produced grain, some a hundredfold, some
> sixty, some thirty.

Some seeds were eaten by the birds, scorched by the sun, and choked by thorns. But the last batch of seeds produced a significant harvest. The seeds Jesus refers to in this parable can apply to individuals and churches as a whole. I most frequently observe the seed falling on the rocky soil. Young leaders grow rapidly but fizzle out because their roots are shallow. It breaks my heart to see how many church leaders simply don't make it for the long haul. The busyness and worries of life hit all of us, and we get worn down from time to time. When our identity is not rooted in Jesus alone, life is simply too hard, frustrating, distracting, and mundane to handle. Very few people finish well.

This is one more reason to first equip people as disciples before placing them in a formal leadership role. We give away titles and leadership roles too easily. Placing people in a formal ministry role too quickly can go downhill fast. We should be watching for faithfulness, consistency, and character before we give people a position or title.

By the grace of God, I have learned from some great mentors who are still walking closely with Jesus after many years. They have helped guide me to structure my life and ministry rhythm for the long haul. But often I catch myself trying to sprint for long periods of time. The harder you sprint, the faster you will wear yourself and others down.

My wife and I laugh about our first year of marriage. Our relationship was great, but I simply ran too hard. She saw warning signs and slowed down. She detected this frantic pace and asked me hard questions I needed to hear. It took me a little while to realize I was heading toward burnout. I used to say, "I'll burn out for Jesus if that's what it takes." This can sound noble, but my wife and four kids wouldn't be too excited about their husband and dad falling victim to self-inflicted ministry carnage.

We all want to leave a mark on this world, but the only way we can sustain a spiritual legacy is by staying connected to Christ regularly and recognizing our limits. He is the Vine, and we are only branches.

I don't mean to be dogmatic here, but I simply don't see a way to keep the roots healthy without the regular practices of Bible reading, prayer, and Sabbath. Without spiritual disciplines and a community of faith around us, we simply cannot sustain growth in Christ for the long haul. Our relationship with God and our discipleship of others will mature only through relationship with God and others.

DISCIPLESHIP AS SPIRITUAL FITNESS

I'm an adrenaline junkie. That's one reason I have to be careful about guarding my energy. I love the challenge of competitive sports and outdoor sports that push my body to the max. I have run a marathon, stuck to conditioning regimens, readied myself for intense mountain climbs, and sometimes just tried to avoid getting the old spare tire. There have been many moments of painful training, when my body didn't want to keep going but my mind forced me to. I will never forget incredible memories of standing on top of mountains, winning championships, and crossing finish lines. Ask any athlete and they will tell you: Victories are won as we train behind the scenes, when no one else is watching.

Of all the workout plans I've had in my life the only ones that lasted were regular. We've all exercised on "the monthly plan" where we visited the gym once a month, worked out hard, felt good about ourselves, and could barely get out of bed for the next three days. It's all pain, no gain. We must view discipleship not as an event but as spiritual fitness. We make our exercise routines regular if we want to see results, and the life of the disciple must be the same. Paul describes the spiritual life as a race: "Do you not know that in a race all the runners run, but only one receives the prize? So run that you may obtain it" (1 Corinthians 9:24). If we want to experience long-lasting growth in Jesus, we must be disciplined.

Unless we are training in righteousness individually and collectively, we will not mature spiritually. At the 2014 Global Leadership Summit, Bill Hybels said, "The culture of a church or organization will only be as healthy as the leader wants it to be." If we aren't modeling a faithful life in Christ, how can we call others into it?

It's easy to look forward to the next Bible study group where we can learn, the next prayer group where we can reconnect to God, the next retreat where we can recalibrate, the next sermon where we can reengage, or the next book where we can get inspired. These are all good things and can be great growth tools, but staying busy with programs and groups in and of themselves will not help you grow in godly character and learn to emulate Jesus. "Supernova Christianity" burns bright and hot, but it fizzles out fast.

As I connect and consult with churches, I see two tracks related to spiritual disciplines. I call the first one "The Spiritual Activity Track."

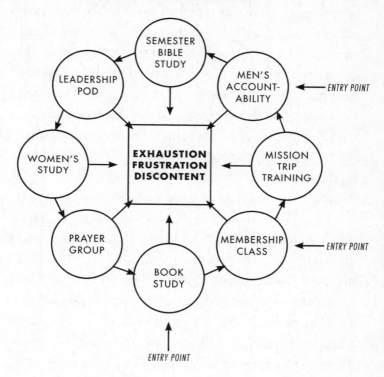

THE SPIRITUAL ACTIVITY TRACK
BUSYNESS WITHOUT TRANSFORMATION

In this track we treat entry points such as Bible studies, small groups, leadership groups, membership classes, book studies, and prayer groups as one stop around the spinning wheel of constant spiritual activity. We are in search of growth, so we simply keep moving. We begin to move around the track to the next group that "fits our needs" for the moment. When a season or semester ends we wonder, *How will I be fed next?*

I've been on this track before. What I experienced and observed from those around me was exhaustion leading to discontent. There was a sinking feeling that there had to be more to life in Jesus than this. My time alone with Jesus grew sparse during this season. I didn't know my neighbors. I wasn't investing in people who didn't know Jesus. My "Sabbath" was jammed with answering e-mails to catch up or get ahead.

Unfortunately people get around this track once or twice and either give up on following the great commission, give up on their church, or give up on the church as a whole. All of these outcomes have this cycle looking less like a wheel and more like the swirling of a flushing toilet.

The "Transformation Track," on the other hand, has discipleship as the core. We learn our identity as God's children, and we grasp the importance of learning, obeying, and reproducing the life of Christ. When we start with a vision to become disciples and to teach others to do likewise, this leads us naturally into a life of mission and away from religious consumption. Life in Christ naturally repurposes us to be ambassadors of Jesus sent to various spheres, cultures, relationships, and neighbors. We realize we are marked for ministry, and we are ready to be sent to make more disciples!

REGULARITY AND COVENANT

Many discipleship groups start with good intentions, but they die out because they are not committed. One person gets "too busy," and then the others begin to realize they have a free pass to miss the group whenever they don't feel like showing up. A few weeks later, you are sitting around with

PROCESS TO PROGRAMS
TRANSFORMATION YIELDING ACTIVITY

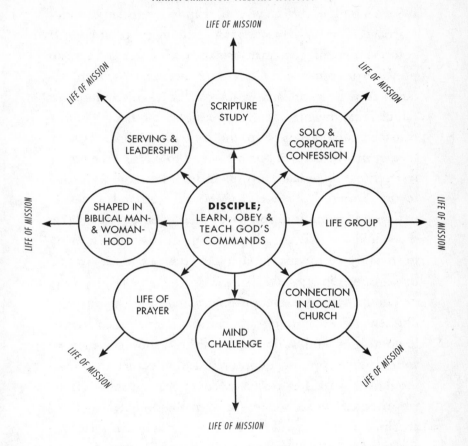

half the group, wondering where everyone is. The group has already died a spiritual death.

The frequency of discipleship group meetings is less important than the regularity of the meetings. In other words, it's better to have a commitment to meet every other week than to say you'll meet every week while lacking the discipline to do so. I have heard of men meeting once or twice a month for fifteen years to shape one another in godly marriage, integrity in business, and walking closer with Jesus. A former apprentice named Ashley decided to lean into the principle of regularity, as God opened her eyes to how important it is to meet regularly with those she was discipling. She noticed that the girls she was meeting with often fell out of the habit of applying Scripture to their lives if they didn't meet regularly. Growth became harder to see, and the group was getting discouraged. So she introduced some regularity to their group. Each week they would read and discuss a passage and commit to apply it to their lives. The next week she would ask how they lived it out. Ashley's discernment to stress regularity made a tangible difference in the lives of these young disciples.

Group leaders must set the stage for consistency and commitment *before* a group starts because it gets much harder to do so later on. I recommend crafting a short covenant as your group is forming. Scripture is full of covenants, so we shouldn't be afraid to craft one. Your covenant should state why the group exists, what is expected of group involvement, and how often you will meet. Our culture breeds a lack of commitment, so calling for commitment will naturally grate against some folks. Ask people to commit to be there unless they are out of town. It might sound too structured at first, but groups with covenants have a much better rate of staying together and multiplying.

Leaders need to be bold and share the commitment

required from the start, or your group will die a slow death of infrequency and inconsistency. Discipleship is a beautiful and rugged journey into living like Jesus. Make sure you plan for the journey before you take off.

DISCUSSION QUESTIONS

In which areas of your life have you seen regularity yield maturity?

What is your weekly spiritual fitness plan?

How are you cultivating spiritual fitness in others?

DISCIPLESHIP MUST BE REPRODUCIBLE

A teacher is one who makes himself progressively unnecessary.
THOMAS CARRUTHERS

Are our methods so simple that the newest believer is employing them? That's how movements multiply disciples, groups and communities of faith. They democratize their methods and allow every follower of Jesus to participate.
STEVE ADDISON

Reproduction is the definitive signal that you are alive!
MIKE BREEN

HAVE YOU EVER HAD someone recognize something special in you? Maybe in a moment they saw a glimmer of something that you didn't see in yourself, and they challenged you. Perhaps you have had people believe in you, promote you, or ask you to join a team you never thought you were qualified for. This was the kind of relationship Paul had to Timothy.

Paul was more than just a teacher to Timothy; he was a spiritual father. Timothy was most likely estranged from his biological father, but Paul saw potential in him. He discipled him, equipped him, challenged him, raised him up to be a pastor, and kept in contact with him. This is the ideal process for spiritual reproduction. These words to Timothy encompass Paul's discipleship process: "What you have heard from me in the presence of many witnesses entrust to faithful men who will be able to teach others also" (2 Timothy 2:2).

Paul's instructions to Timothy are clear: What you have seen and heard from me should be offered as a gift to others. Missionaries call this the 2.2.2 principle, a plan for four generations of discipleship from the start: the discipler, the disciple, those the disciple entrusts with the message, and those who then hear the message. Kingdom leaders intentionally plant the seed of the gospel and challenge others to reproduce it. Discipleship is not something to be comprehended and mastered but something to be lived out and passed on to others. We are not simply receivers of discipleship but transceivers of it.

The 2.2.2 principle is simple, but I missed it for years. I was a little slow on the uptake. It must become common practice in the church today. Every follower of Jesus has the capacity to become a multiplier of the message.

CHURCH PLANTING AND REPRODUCIBILITY

The things we measure say a lot about us. As the adage goes, "What gets celebrated gets done." Reproducible discipleship looks beyond numbers to count generations—it measures how many disciples have made disciples.

A man named Ying Kai set out to disciple with this generational mind-set. His format for discipling included multiplication of disciples as a priority. He can now point to seventeen generations of people who follow Christ and disciple others. Talk about the 2.2.2 principle at work! When we aim at mere numbers, we will rarely multiply disciples, but when we aim at generations, numbers come naturally.[1]

I am hearing more church planters launching with a vision to plant future churches already in place. They are planting pregnant! Believe it or not, churches of around two hundred folks are more likely to plant new churches than churches of a thousand.[2] This seems counterintuitive. I believe this is primarily because of the reproducibility factor: The smaller the church system, the easier it is to maintain and thus to reproduce. Small churches often have bivocational pastors who don't require a full salary, so the financial paradigm is more reproducible as well. It is also less intimidating to think about planting a small or midsized church than sustaining a large one. The bar for excellence is often more realistic at a smaller church. Leading a large church requires a diversity and capacity of leadership that simply isn't realistic for most pastors. Moreover, a church that plants pregnant has a vision beyond itself, one that celebrates multiplication and seeks to develop it on multiple levels.

Don't get me wrong. I love churches of all sizes and flavors. Some leaders have the capacity to lead large churches. I am not anti-megachurch. I interact with many large churches that are leveraging what God has given them to multiply churches and new networks. Many are doing this effectively. Big churches often have the potential to place someone on staff for a season as a resident church planter and to send them with care and financial support. Many large churches are launching microchurches that contextualize the gospel in a new place without having to re-create structures, processes, and vision. Big churches can be very effective. But on the whole, big churches are a rare occurrence.

As a church grows, its leaders need to be on guard not to become so focused on the growth that they lose the desire to multiply. I often hear something like this: "Someday we will plant churches when we have a thousand people to spare" or "Someday we will plant churches when we have the money" or "Someday we will be ready to send some of our best leaders out." It rarely works that way. It's like saying, "When I'm making $100,000 a year, I'll start being generous." I'm all for making a good plan so your equipping and planting processes are well structured, but maybe your church should multiply sooner than you think. There will always be another excuse. Start taking steps toward multiplication of disciples and leaders today, and maybe tomorrow you will be ready to start planting churches or at least partnering with a church-planting network in a significant way.

There are, indeed, some churches that should be on birth control. When couples aren't emotionally healthy, it makes sense to focus on strengthening the relationship and creating a healthy home before expanding the family. It's not a "never" but a "not now." They need to get healthy before multiplying. Similarly, some churches aren't ready to directly plant a church from their church. There are plenty of opportunities for legacy churches like these to partner with a new or healthy congregation or to gift their building to another congregation. In fact, when we understand multiplication of ministry as a sign of health, a church will grow in its desire to multiply disciples, leaders, and churches and will be ready to plant when the time comes. One thing I have observed many times: God blesses churches when they are openhanded.

In the meantime, churches in the process of getting healthy might support a new church plant through finances, prayer support, lending their building, or meeting other tangible needs. You have to start somewhere. Take the first right step. Church planting churches don't need to be perfect, just healthy and generous.

ONE IN A MILLION VERSUS A MILLION IN ONE

In his book *The E-Myth Revisited,* Michael Gerber says that every business model "will be operated by people with the lowest possible level of skill."[3] He calls this the "Law of Ordinary People." This law is central to reproducibility. When we portray discipleship as complicated (even unknowingly), ordinary people leave discipleship to the experts, and reproduction is killed before it starts. We should be modeling and imparting simple and achievable discipleship processes without lowering the bar of commitment.

There is a subtle lie floating around that the church simply needs to function like a not-for-profit knockoff of Jim Collins's business bestseller *Good to Great.* While key principles can be gleaned from the business world, not everything translates to ministry. Reproducibility can be death to businesses—if your idea is overly reproducible, other companies may take your idea and steal some of your market share. In the upside-down Kingdom of God, however, this is exactly what we are going for! We *want* people to steal our best practices. We *want* our message to be passed on easily.

We *want* people to do what we're doing in their own context. Steal, borrow, and copy ideas as long as it is genuine to the context. There is no market share when it comes to discipleship, only stewardship of the best gift on the planet.

We have been entrusted with an extraordinary message. As Paul told Timothy, we are charged with the responsibility to pass that extraordinary message on to ordinary receivers, who will then impart it to others. This is inherently multiplicative: One carrier can convey a message that is passed on to millions. If it can be remembered and passed on at a moment's notice, it is reproducible. Experts are one in a million, but reproducible messages are a million in one.

CONFERENCED OUT

I talk with leaders nearly every week who are conferenced out. They just don't want to attend one more national conference. I can identify with them. You get fired up taking a journal full of notes from leaders whose churches "made it." You strategize how you will implement their model in your church. Sometime between the plane ride and pulling into your driveway, you get a deep sense of angst. You share this on Monday with your leadership team, and they aren't excited about it. Then the postconference depression sets in.

Ministry conferences can be incredible spaces to hear from solid practitioners; we even host a conference annually. But the reproducibility factor from such gatherings tends to be low. The experts presenting their model in settings like this didn't get there overnight, but a conference setting doesn't allow for the whole story, only the high points. We should take into account a couple of factors when seeking to reproduce what we hear at a conference in our own setting.

Ability. The talent of the leaders rising to the surface of the church today can be downright intimidating. Most of the time, it's simply not realistic to compare ourselves to those leaders who seem to have effortlessly experienced "success." A model that is dependent on an extremely high ability level is not very reproducible. God gets no glory when we compare ourselves to others, and anything that is expert-centric violates Gerber's law of ordinary people.

Context. There is no singular model of disciple-making ministry, but there are missionary principles we can follow. Harlem is different from Portland, so the flavor of our discipleship in these different contexts must be different also. Effective models are formed through the old-fashioned hard work of learning your community and adapting your methods. Taking shortcuts around contextualization rarely works. If a model presented at a conference is dependent on a specific context, it is not very reproducible.

EPIC SUCCESS?

After a blog post that caught a lot of unexpected attention, my brother, J. R. Briggs, decided to host a different kind of gathering, called Epic Fail Pastors Conference. He envisioned pastors gathering to share how they were *actually* doing in ministry, pushing past the pleasantries and perceived perfection. He dreamed of a space to celebrate faithfulness instead of "success." Surprisingly, people came from many different states—even continents—and beautiful things surfaced.

Instead of epic wins, people shared character-shaping "failures." They shared as learners, not experts, and as such, the insights that emerged were incredibly reproducible.[4] Blogs, articles, tweets, discussions, and meetings about this idea have surfaced throughout the United States and have been adapted into smaller roundtables in different contexts to fit different needs. Leaders have gathered to share deeply and to center themselves on the gospel in spaces ranging from seminaries to a church-building-turned-bar to a decommissioned Catholic church. Dare I say these reproducible events have been an "epic success"?

David Garrison, a specialist on global church-planting movements, looks for common elements of God movements all over the world. The stories he shares of Muslims coming to faith in Jesus are nothing short of amazing. David challenges each disciple to ask the "WIGTake" question: "What's it gonna take to see a movement?" "Unless you can train lots of co-laborers," he says, "your dreams will never become a reality."[5] A tool or system won't spread if it can't be passed easily through regular people, using regular systems on a regular basis. If something is too specialized, it will be too limited for the masses. If you hear people saying, "I can do that too!" it's a great sign. Reproducibility can create a culture of inspiration and empowerment around you. Our eyes and our prayers should be focused on those we can equip for faithful ministry.

Everyone is brilliant in his or her own way. Everyone's a genius! We each can do something that seems completely natural to us while others watch and say, "I could never do that." This is what happens when my friend busts out his

DISCIPLESHIP MUST BE REPRODUCIBLE

dance moves at a wedding reception. I don't understand how a body moves like that. I promptly exit stage left to "go find the dessert table." We understand when a level of excellence is beyond our reach, and we remain passive. We must be wary of creating performance-based ministry systems that will cause people to go find the dessert table.

I am a big fan of teaching teams in churches and am honored to be part of one. Not only are they great breeding grounds for developing teachers, communicating the fullness of the body of Christ, and empowering new leaders, but they also take leaders down from the pedestal. While excellence and giftedness are important to preaching and teaching, we should be looking for potential giftedness in teaching paired with faithfulness.

Remember the farm-system model of developing leaders instead of simply importing them? Most churches I interact with have not developed a team but a list of substitutes to communicate the gospel. There is a big difference between substitute teachers and guest speakers. Think back to middle school. When a substitute teacher was sitting in the teacher's desk before class, I prepared for busywork, a boring movie, or goofing off. Everyone knew that the substitute was there only because the teacher was away. In contrast, when one of my teachers brought in a guest speaker, we waited with expectation because we knew they offered something unique.

We can experience this same dynamic in the church. When you set up a substitute model, your church experiences a letdown when the lead pastor does not teach. Conversely, teaching teams allow people begin to see the power of the gospel expressed through a team of people. Over the past several years our church has moved from having substitute teachers to having a teaching team. A fairly diverse group has gelled into a team. People who are passionate about learning to teach or exhibit a potential teaching gift are invited to audit the team. We all have different passions, different stories, different ministry focuses, and different voices. It is a joy to be part of a diverse teaching team, where God speaks through many mouths, all of whom are growing in their craft. Perhaps your church needs to embark on the journey from substitute teachers to a teaching team.

GOING SMALL

Talented leaders and teachers tend to attract large groups. There is nothing wrong with this. The masses wanted to listen to Jesus and watch him do miracles; few wanted to be sent out on his mission, and even fewer dropped their lives and gave everything for the call. While I love large gatherings, they are the least reproducible things churches do. Many new churches begin with small monthly or biweekly worship gatherings in order to put more focus on discipleship in other venues. Some churches even like this rhythm so much that they have chosen a bimonthly worship gathering, with home gatherings on the alternate weeks.

Focused equipping gatherings have a high potential for reproducibility, as do other small gatherings, such as small groups, missional communities, discipleship huddles, and life-transformation groups (LTGs). Ed Stetzer sees this potential for reproducibility in effective small groups:

In human growth, multiplication allows the cell to become multiple cells, which allow change and growth to occur. Similarly, for growth to occur in the church, people groups must continuously grow and multiply. Smaller groups are more easily multiplied than larger groups.[6]

When done with mission and intention, small gatherings can harness a unique power among God's people. There are four advantages I see in utilizing smaller gatherings for discipleship.

- *Shared leadership.* If the structure is simple enough, the group can be led by many different people.
- *Leadership development.* They provide great environments for developing new leaders through relational and experiential learning.
- *Sustainability.* They can be sustained with minimal burden, so they have great potential for longevity.
- *Multiplication.* With some intention and planning, they can lead to new groups. The churches that are seeing multiplication from their small groups launch with apprentice leaders and an intentional focus on gospel expansion.

I like to train leaders in smaller settings where discussion and reflection is expected. I often choose to run a group focused on equipping for a short period of time, with a pre-determined termination date for the group. That way, each person in the group can start a group of his or her own, even before the group ends. I will share more about this process in later chapters.

SUBTRACTING TO MULTIPLY

Jesus did ministry with fewer people in order to reach more people. Jesus sent seventy-two people out on his mission with only a small dose of training (see Luke 10). He trained twelve in his small group (including Judas, whom Matthias replaced in Acts 1). He had only three people in his inner ring. Jesus let Peter, James, and John closer to the action and closer to himself than the others. He shared several personal, watershed moments with just them: They saw Jairus's daughter healed (Mark 5:37-42), Jesus' transfiguration (Mark 9:2-3), and Jesus' most vulnerable moments in Gethsemane (Mark 14:33). Of the three, Jesus seemed to share a special affinity with John, which is why we refer to John as "the disciple whom Jesus loved."

This was Jesus' leadership development plan: In order to multiply, Jesus subtracted from seventy-two to twelve to three to one.

Paul had a similar inner ring. While he had a huge network of friends and supporters, he had a smaller group of comrades and an even smaller group of co-laborers with whom he shared the deepest ministry connection. There are somewhere around one hundred people mentioned in Acts and the Epistles whom Paul was associated with. He refers to thirty-six of them with terms such as *brother*, *apostle*, *fellow workers*, and *servant*. Of these, Paul mentioned only nine coworkers with whom he was closely associated.[7] This inner ring of nine appears to have been more fruitful disciple-makers. He even referred to Timothy as "my true child in the faith" (1 Timothy 1:2).

Since Paul was a traveling spiritual entrepreneur, he needed to train lots of leaders to strengthen the church around and behind him. In order to multiply, Paul subtracted from a hundred to thirty-six to nine to one.

Ying Kai, perhaps the most fruitful disciple-maker in the world today, has been faithfully making disciples who make disciples in China for many years. He and his wife have been tirelessly starting groups and training ordinary people to see extraordinary movements of God. Millions of disciples can be traced back to Ying and his wife! They are training people with the hope that they all become exponential multipliers, but they have experienced that around one in every five they train experiences deep fruitful discipleship.

When you crunch the numbers, you find the inner ring of fruitful disciples to be almost exactly the same for Jesus, Paul, and Ying Kai: three out of twelve for Jesus, nine out of thirty-six for Paul, and one out of five for Ying—a range of 20 to 25 percent each. It was fascinating to uncover this similarity. Can we predict who our own 20 to 25 percent will be? No. We don't know who is going to reproduce the gospel with fruitfulness. So our only response is to train hungry people and watch what God does through them. Ying says, "God chooses the person. We never know. Don't choose. Train everyone! Then let God choose."[8]

In order to multiply we must subtract, but we must also

invest. We must cast a vision for disciples who make disciples who make disciples.

DISCUSSION QUESTIONS

Are you experiencing fruit from your discipleship efforts two, three, or four generations down the line? Why or why not?

Is your church on the transformation track or the spiritual activity track? How do you know?

What initial steps can your church take toward planting new churches?

Who is your inner ring?

DISCIPLESHIP MUST BE POSITIVE

Frustrated people generally don't start movements—but sometimes they do start wars.
BOB ROBERTS JR.

Most people do not see the local church as a place to achieve greatness.
DAVID MURROW

Am I a part of the cure? Or am I part of the disease?
COLDPLAY

WHY DO GUYS ALWAYS STOP *showing up for these groups?*
I started asking myself this question late in college. I knew there was something bigger at work than pure fatigue. A few friends and I had begun asking how we would serve Jesus for the rest of our lives. These were good men, some of the most dedicated I've ever seen at this age. We just couldn't figure out why all this passion and dedication didn't result in greater commitment to our group. Even with the best intentions, negativity always managed to creep in the back door of our lives and sour our groups.

The problem was too close to our faces to recognize. We were like fish trying to describe water.

This chapter was born out of experiencing the pain of groups disbanding without significant impact. I have created many environments where I unconsciously tried to motivate others through self-reliance, shame, and guilt. I wish I had learned the principle of positivity earlier. I have come to realize that shame-based discipleship is not discipleship at all; it's an attempt at behavior modification.

Shame has been our default setting since the Garden of Eden. We often try to start our discipleship paradigm with a negative perspective. We think that if we just had a handle on a few sins, we would finally line up, and finally our lives would look more like Jesus'. Don't get me wrong: Sins get a foothold in our lives and hold us back from pursuing the fullness of God. Lust, pride, envy, and self-reliance are just a few of the vices destroying the church today, and we simply cannot ignore them. But we need to face the fact that sin management simply doesn't work. It may work temporarily to relieve a specific sin, but without our faces turned toward God and the power of the Holy Spirit in us, our attempts at growth simply won't last. As we seek mutual accountability in our discipleship, we shouldn't aim to rid one another of sin but to pursue godliness together.

We live in a busted-up world, where injustice is far too prevalent and our places are full of cracks. Social issues are in our faces today. Globalization and technology have brought issues from halfway across the globe to our smartphones. But in the midst of all of these things, one of the things that disturbs me the most is that many Christians are taking a posture of guarding instead of blessing, throwing grenades instead of loving others. Blessing others is not about agreeing with everything in their lives; it's about loving them as Jesus would. Let's not get so distracted about bad news in this world that we forget there is good news.

The gospel is good news because it doesn't depend on our goodness but on God's. There *is* carnage in this world. We *are* weak. We *are* sinners. We *are* in need of grace. But that's only half the story. Let's not forget that we have been *rescued* from our sins and *saved* from ourselves, and we can experience *freedom*. We need to stop thinking like losers. In the end, we win!

Recently I was part of an event seeking to equip Christ followers to incarnate the gospel through being more present as neighbors. Groups walked neighborhoods, listened to developing stories, and dreamed about what could be. Instead of putting the focus on the cracks in our city as the evening news does, we focused on another story. I was amazed by the alternative story that God is writing through his people.

Negativity is not attractive. Hate, excessive critique, and negativity aren't winsome. Joy, crafting beauty, and hope are winsome. We must choose wisely.

We are not bound to the half of the story that our world hears. The main story dominates our thinking and ignores our victory in Christ. We simply cannot afford to become so distracted by the main story that we miss the alternate story.

Ashley, a former apprentice I mentioned earlier, brought hope to those she led by focusing on the alternate story God was writing in their lives. After recognizing her accidental focus on the story of shame and negativity, she felt freed to focus on encouraging instead of disapproving. Her role now hinged on bringing life to the group by focusing on the victories those girls were sharing and reminding them of the promises of God. The tone of her group completely changed. The girls were no longer viewing their group through the fear and insecurity of what they lacked but through the riches they had received through Christ. Staying positive kept her group alive. Perhaps you lead a group that needs to focus on the alternative story God is crafting.

WHAT WE'RE FOR OR WHAT WE'RE AGAINST?

Most people's views of Christians are based on what we're against. This is a sad reality and a sign that we have taken a wrong turn. The church is to be a dash of salt and a beam of light to a longing world. We can't just have an anti-identity like a stubborn, angry teenager with arms crossed, swearing not to sell out to "the man" or to act like his old man. Anti-identities repel people. Those of us who call Jesus Lord need to be *for* what Jesus is for: freedom, grace, life to the fullest, compassion, seeing the lost be found, serving our communities, becoming strong dads and loving moms, and seeing heaven come to earth. If you follow Jesus, you are called to be an advocate, not a curmudgeon.

In his first letter to the Corinthians, Paul approaches a hot topic in an unusual way. When addressing the subject of sexual immorality, a topic rampant in our culture today, he leads us to the positive. "You are not your own, for you were bought with a price. So glorify God in your body" (1 Corinthians 6:19-20). Much contemporary teaching on Christian sexuality tends toward the negative, but notice how Paul frames his teaching: His opening observation, "All things are lawful for me" (1 Corinthians 6:12), echoes his broad message of freedom (see Galatians, for example) and is consistent with Jesus' teaching on the Sabbath as "made for man" (Mark 2:27), whom Jesus came to offer life "abundantly" (John 10:10).

Throughout his ministry Jesus focused on what is helpful and designed by God instead of what is merely lawful. Jesus even chastised the Pharisees for their empty hearts behind their perfection in keeping the Sabbath. Rather than guarding against the negative, Paul follows Jesus' lead and makes a positive, logical argument for a biblical sexual ethic that God has designed us for.

By the end of Paul's treatise on sexuality, we don't feel constrained but instead released to live in godliness. Paul ends by telling us, "You are not your own, for you were bought with a price"—essentially telling us we have become slaves—and yet this still manages to come across as a message of freedom. He challenges the Corinthians to something bigger than themselves: a life glorifying to God.

How would it change the groups and churches we lead if we aimed at glorifying God instead of managing sin? People would leave drenched in grace and freedom, yet challenged toward living in the way of Jesus.

As simple as the positivity principle is, it's absent in most of our discipleship processes. How often we forget that our debts have been paid by Jesus and that a great banquet feast awaits us. Our groups should reflect the life and freedom Christ came to bring.

TRASH DUMPING

A former apprentice, Matt, was deeply challenged by this principle of positivity. "Especially as a guy," he told me, "one of the things that was so easy for me to do in a deep spiritual relationship was to dump all my trash and sin on another person. I was an excellent trash dumper, and my relationships suffered because of that."

Matt experienced freedom as he began to see how Jesus dealt with the trash in people's lives. The trash was never Jesus' focus. Jesus wanted to heal them of the sins eating up their freedom, but he didn't dwell on their sins. We want to see those we are discipling grow and be freed from their sin, but growth involves so much more than trash dumping.

We all are tempted to approach others in a posture of negativity. Often we are more comfortable creating the friction of iron sharpening iron than encouraging godliness. Iron sharpening iron, as we see in Proverbs 27:17, is not wrong. In fact God matures us through it. The danger is when people abuse this verse to challenge each other under the label of "accountability." Another apprentice was honest enough to confess what many of us have done: "I have been extremely good at managing my sin. I have been really good at using 'Christianese' to make myself feel superior and make others think about what *they* need to work on. I have not always focused on spurring others on to good works and love."

This is not how God designed discipleship. What if the questions we asked one another led us to life instead of death?

People come to me a lot to vent about church issues.

Usually they are simply relational issues, but the other person just happens to be part of a church family. After listening to their grievances I ask, "Are you willing to be part of the solution?" This is a huge indicator of whether they are rock throwers or problem solvers.

Rock throwers are not burdened to help a person, church, or group mature; they just want to smash a few windows and run. Problem solvers, by contrast, are the kind of people every church family needs. They start by asking questions because they are burdened to be part of the solution. How do you know the difference? Wait and see how they respond.

Often God lets us see unhealthiness or issues so we can be positive agents of change. However, if we aren't interested in being part of the solution, we need to practice the discipline of silence. Rock throwers who aren't prepared to be problem solvers should wait and pray about how to approach the issue as a potential part of the solution. Until they commit themselves to that discipline, they can be poison to those around them and to their church communities. In my experience, unless rock throwers learn to engage a community through discipling relationships, they will go to the church down the street and start throwing rocks there.

I am not suggesting we pretend our lives are all rosy after we trust Jesus. I'm not talking about quaint answers to a life of false pretense or outward illusions. I'm not talking about avoiding hard conversations about sin. I'm talking about keeping an appropriate posture of gratefulness to God.

My friend Kelly talks a lot about the distinction of "raw" versus "real." Rawness tends to rub someone the wrong way, dump some trash on them, and drop the mic. Realness, by contrast, is transparent and healthy. Some folks want to complain about how God isn't speaking to them, blessing them, caring for them, or helping them. I realize we all experience dry times and seasons when we feel distant from God. When someone appears to be in one of these seasons, I like to ask him or her, "How are you submitting to God during this storm?" or "What sacrifices are you willing to make in order to experience freedom?" This can help you gauge whether they have a positive spark and whether they have a desire to grow or simply want to relax in the land of mediocrity.

We should have unexplainable joy as Christians. We were once shipwrecked, and now we stand on dry land! I was once drowning in the sea of myself, but now my life is defined by Jesus. On my worst day, when my best simply wasn't good enough for those around me, I can relax because it isn't about me.

We have the best news in the entire world, but if we are leading people with a leash of shame, we've missed the gospel. We must seek to cultivate those around us toward deeper relationships with God. As we encourage and challenge the people we are leading toward learning Jesus with us, they will learn his liberating message.

START WITH THE END IN MIND
Jesus wasn't interested in pointing out people's dirty laundry except when it came to the pride of the Pharisees. While we don't want to "pick our poison" when it comes to sin, I believe that the chains the Pharisees were carrying were the heaviest around, like a boulder anchoring their souls to the bottom of the sea.

No one starts with the intention of a discipleship group going south, but if the aim is off by just a few degrees, we will miss the target. "How did you screw up this week?" isn't discipleship; it's sin management. Who will keep showing up to a group like this?

I have struggled through and eventually quit my fair share of groups because they lacked life. The guys in these groups started making new excuses each week, and some just stopped showing up altogether. We weren't growing closer to God; we were only growing discouraged. Eventually I jumped off the ship too. When groups end like this, there is always something going on under the surface. John Ortberg dissects the spiritual progression that takes place in a group that lacks positivity in a "cycle of religious enslavement."[1]

THE CYCLE OF
RELIGIOUS ENSLAVEMENT

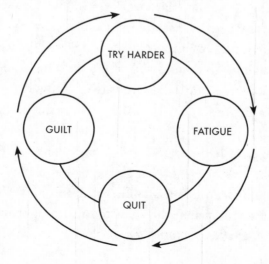

Now let's turn this progression toward shame on its head. Have you ever been part of a group that was like fresh water for your soul? These are the times when you cancel whatever you had scheduled in order to show up. I had one of these evenings recently where five of us were reminding one another about God's goodness in contrast to our shortcomings. A man recently told me he woke up at 4:00 a.m. and couldn't get back to sleep because he was so excited for our discipleship breakfast. God met him that day with grace and affirmation through a group of dudes eating the Early Bird Special together. These spaces let us experience what spurring one another on toward love and good deeds feels like. We will gladly confess our sins one to another in beautiful vulnerability, giving us all an opportunity to "gospel" one another.

A simple rephrasing of our questions can help guide our groups. Consider starting with questions such as "How did you experience victory this week?" or "How did God show you freedom?" or "What glimpses did you catch of God's Kingdom?" or "What are you celebrating?" or "How did God use your failure to remind you of grace?" Our accountability questions can be similarly positive: "How did you glorify God this week?" or "In which areas is sin stealing your freedom?"

If you have had negative group experiences in the past, you might even want to change the name of the group. If "accountability group" has come to mean "beat-down session," you might change the name to something that embodies growth, challenge, and freedom.

The gospel is the best thing that's ever happened to me. I tell people, "You will get to the end of me in fifteen minutes, and then you'll get to Jesus." Once we get past small talk, you will find Jesus hiding out in every area of my life. Charles Spurgeon talked about all roads in Scripture leading to Jesus; all roads in our lives should do the same. We have just a short time here on this earth, and we have limited time and energy. I want to be part of groups that rejoice in the finished work of Christ, not groups that dwell on the unfinished work in me. I want to be part of a movement, not a critique. I want to proclaim and embody the life-changing gospel with those hearing it for the first time and to share it again with those who need to be reminded.

DISCUSSION QUESTIONS

In which areas of your life are you carrying shame instead of freedom?

Are you more of a rock thrower or a problem solver in your church family?

What can you do to create more positivity in your discipleship processes?

APPLYING MOVEMENT PRINCIPLES

Movements happen when people who thought they were alone find out that they are not.
TIM SOERENS

As a catalyst, it's all about letting go and trusting the community.
ORI BRAFMAN

He who loves his dream of a community more than the Christian community itself becomes a destroyer of the latter.
DIETRICH BONHOEFFER

IN ACTS 4, THE CHURCH is exploding by the thousands in Jerusalem. The religious authorities aren't happy that Peter and John are preaching Jesus as Lord and healing the lame, so they arrest them and take them into custody. When publicly questioned, Peter deflects praise back to Jesus.

> Rulers of the people and elders, if we are being examined today concerning a good deed done to a crippled man, by what means this man has been healed, let it be known to all of you and to all the people of Israel that by the name of Jesus Christ of Nazareth, whom you crucified, whom God raised

from the dead—by him this man is standing before you well. This Jesus is the stone that was rejected by you, the builders, which has become the cornerstone. And there is salvation in no one else, for there is no other name under heaven given among men by which we must be saved.

ACTS 4:8-12

Here's what Peter is saying.

- Jesus healed the crippled man through us.
- Jesus was rejected by the religious authorities, crucified, and raised from the dead.
- Jesus is the only way to eternal life.

Peter delivers the perfect three-point gospel sermon here, and it doesn't even have any alliteration.

The next verse should rock us to the core. "Now when they saw the boldness of Peter and John, and perceived that they were uneducated, common men, they were astonished. And they recognized that they had been with Jesus" (Acts 4:13). It's as if they're saying, "We see God has transformed them—there's no other way they'd be that bold on their own!"

Can people notice you have been with Jesus? Can others see transformation in your life? If I could be a fly on the wall at my funeral, I hope people would say I was an ordinary dude who had unmistakably been with Jesus. That's it. Then they can bring out the brisket and strike up the bluegrass band.

Movements of God have been popping up all over the globe, from China to South America to Iran. While I don't claim to be an expert in movements, I'm an observer of them. Many of these movements are taking place among uneducated, common men and women with no seminary training and limited access to biblical study tools. In many cases, because of religious persecution, their only option is to meet in house churches under the cover of night. Sometimes these groups have only pages ripped from a Bible that they study for days before trading with another house church. Christians go from these meetings back to their own villages, sharing the liberating love of Jesus with their whole circle of relationships. When their friends, family, and neighbors come to know Jesus, they teach them all they know and encourage them to go tell others this Good News immediately. The risk is much greater than anything we face. What God is doing through these ordinary people is nothing short of astonishing.

In environments like these, it's easy to see the six movement principles at work.

It's really *simple* because, due to persecution, they don't have the luxury of complexity.

It's *holistic* because they have made a radical life change that will cost them in every area of their lives.

It's *adaptable* because their models change as they share Christ in new places. They meet without even the whole of Scripture in homes and secret places.

It's *regular* because they are meeting as often as they can to pray, worship, and train in godliness so they can tell others of this great gospel. They have no other choice than to be the church all week.

It's *reproducible* because it is traveling quickly through towns and villages. The proof is in the pudding. There is a quick turnaround time from first hearing the gospel to training others to share the gospel.

It's *positive* because they share how this gospel breaks chains, liberates the lost, and brings freedom even amid earthly persecution.

We have no reason to look at these movement makers and say, "I can't do that." Movements spread through common people who have been transformed by Jesus. Steve Addison says, "Movements change people, and changed people change the world."[1] God seems to be using ordinary people today who have been changed by Jesus. It's not about impressive résumés; it's about faithfulness and courage.

The age of the impressive leader is bending the knee to the age of the transformed servant. People want to follow people who have been transformed by Jesus. If push comes to shove, we must be willing to trade a pedestal for a towel, a book contract for a team of hungry leaders, a role on a church staff for our families following Jesus. If we want to see God movements, we need to equip and unleash people who rely on the power of Jesus.

Is there power in the gospel you are living? Perhaps a powerless gospel can explain why most churches are in decline, why Christians are widely viewed as judgmental, and why pastors are flocking away from the ministry. My friend Peyton Jones told me, "It's as if we are looking for any possible solution other than total dependence on God." We can have all the structure, strategy, and ideas we want, but if we aren't in love with Jesus and resolved to do whatever God wants, it will all fall short.

We must recover the saltiness and the glow that Jesus alone can give us. This astonishing power doesn't come from sitting in a pew or attending a weekly Bible study. It doesn't come from higher education. It doesn't come from leading a gospel community or adopting a local school. It comes from the transforming power of Jesus alone. Our world is dying to see people who are lit ablaze by Jesus and released into the world. When we become less and Jesus becomes more, it will soon be evident that we are nothing special, but that we carry something that has changed the trajectory of our lives. Perhaps God is seen most clearly when he is doing extraordinary work through very ordinary people.

BE A CHEATER

I'll be completely honest here. When I began to apply the six principles for a multiplying church outlined in this book, it felt too good to be true, as if I were cheating. I was straining less but experiencing more fruit. Before I applied these principles, the burdensome discipleship processes I had learned had been heavy and hard to maintain, and the people I was discipling were depending on me to sustain them. In the past, if I was sick or out of town, groups I led either didn't meet or struggled. Groups I led were accidentally focused around my personality, and any growth was by addition, not multiplication. If Christ gives us a light burden to carry, if it is for freedom that Christ set us free, why don't our ministries reflect that?

Don't get me wrong; discipleship will always take work and require time and energy. Co-laboring with Christ isn't something to take lightly. But there is a difference between hard work and frustration. If you find yourself constantly stressed, behind, cynical, and exhausted as you're seeking to make disciples and raise up leaders, maybe you need a better framework for living out the mission of God. The ministry treadmill is exhausting.

To apply these six principles, you will have to leave much of what you know behind and cling to Jesus. It took about six months of practicing these principles in three different groups to be convinced this framework was here to stay. I took notes during group times when one of the principles was embodied. When I looked over a semester of notes, I saw that all six were essential. Without fail they would come up. Each week, guys couldn't wait to show up to the group and were genuinely frustrated when they couldn't attend. This was a far cry from the "free skips" and "no-call, no-shows" I had experienced in the past. Joining God's mission can be hard, but God actually does much of the heavy lifting.

While I am trying hard to steer away from talking about a model, these principles have worked their way into a format that has proven very effective. Please know that within these segments you will need to adapt to the Spirit. No meeting time will be exactly the same. In what follows, I will lay out what has been effective in our context, but you will most likely need to adapt it. For example, I live in a very transient city because of military life, missions training, and colleges. Our groups usually have very little intro time and must move very quickly to the multiplication stage. It might not need to go quite so fast in your context. I also sense a unique call to retrain folks who are already in some kind of ministry but are struggling to find guardrails. Your context may not be so saturated with people already involved in ministry.

GROUP DYNAMICS

Expectations are crucial to discipleship. There are a few crucial things to start with.

- Hunger in those you are inviting into a group.
- Commitment, from you and them, to continue meeting for a certain amount of time and to be part of leading some of the group times.
- A commitment to start discipling others by the time this group is over.

This third qualification reinforces the importance of reproduction in discipleship. I limit my groups to between three and five people in order to keep them reproducible and relational—just as Jesus invested in Peter, James, and John so that they would be equipped to multiply the gospel among many others. You're going to need to subtract in order to multiply.

My favorite venue for discipling men is around a table at a local breakfast joint, but choose what fits for your group. I rotate the role of group leader starting in the first week so that everyone learns group leadership experientially. This also allows the group to revolve around the gospel and the great commission, not around you, the discipler. In fact, in my first three groups, I had to miss at least one week of each. My absence made for a good litmus test for reproducibility: If your group runs effectively on a week when you're not there, it's heading in the right direction.

I meet with my groups for around ninety minutes, often before work. Our agendas for each meeting are divided into three parts, with thirty minutes for each section. Don't get so focused on the clock that you forget to listen to the Spirit.

Section 1: Look back. This is a time to reflect on the group's previous time together. The group leader shepherds the group during this time. It's natural to start a group time hearing how others are doing, just as you would at a lunch meeting. This should be more intentional, however, than asking, "How was your week?" Ideally each person takes notes each week on what the others are sharing, so they can pray for them throughout the week and ask them about progress next week. If someone commits to an action step one week, make sure to follow up on it the next week, and see how God used that action step to grow them. If you skip this step, your group members might accomplish things and grow, but they will not experience connected relationships that will outlast your group. You can ask questions such as the following:

- What victories did you experience this week?
- How did you see God at work?

- In which areas have you been resisting God?
- Which Scripture from last week came to light during the week?

Section 2: Look up. This section is about hearing from God through Scripture and prayer. I almost always start these groups by focusing on the Sermon on the Mount. Not only is this passage foundational to Jesus' life and ministry, but it takes nearly every area of life into account. Group members can immediately turn around and lead people of varying maturity levels through this passage of Scripture.

Groups that are designed for discipleship but never get around to praying and reading Scripture are eventually just hangouts. They usually have a short shelf life because they lack the power of the Spirit, don't have a clear purpose, and become stale. There is certainly a time for these spaces in your life—as long as you are not expecting deep growth or time in Scripture. On the other hand, groups that are focused only on prayer and Scripture can lack the relational and experiential learning that is crucial for true discipleship to take root. Relationship is vital to discipleship!

I have noticed that those who are slower processors will learn a lot from others sharing but won't talk much during the group time. This is fine. Trust God to teach them what he wants them to learn.

You will need to resist the urge to simply teach. This was a struggle for me at first. There is certainly a space for teaching within groups, but this is not the space for it. You are the leader, but you are also a learner. As learners in our groups, we read through Scripture passages together, looking for things that stick out or that we have questions about. Typically those questions are answered by looking back to Scripture and sharing insights with one another.

Resist the urge to cover too much Scripture. The beauty here comes in slowly digesting words or topics that you have skipped over before. The facilitator for the week can keep the time on track.

Ask questions such as the following:

- What are you seeing in this Scripture passage that you have never seen before?
- Which verse is God highlighting for you?
- Why is this verse so impactful?
- What is God speaking to you in this moment?

Section 3: Look ahead. Most discipleship groups and Bible studies never look ahead or give any kind of challenge. So this section will likely be your biggest adjustment. We study Scripture not merely to be informed about God but to be formed by him. You will have to keep reminding people that the point of your time together is not cognition but hearing and responding to God. Human nature is to resist challenge. Make sure you ask each person to share something they will do each week in response to God's leading. Some of the responses in groups I've led have blown me away.

Often accountability groups hold members accountable to what group members have challenged them to do, but we need to hold each other accountable to what God has challenged us to do. In this section we are asking, sometimes digging, for a response to the Spirit's leading.

During this "look ahead" time, I ask group members to pray for three people—their "top three"—whom they can invite into a discipling relationship that follows a similar process. Each week it's important to ask whom specifically God is putting on their hearts. When he does, our task becomes to hold one another accountable to taking the plunge and inviting that person into a discipling process. I've found that unless we hold people's feet to the fire on this issue while our group is still meeting, the chances of them discipling others are greatly reduced. I have a friend who even disbanded a discipleship group with pastors because they had agreed to multiply a group of their own, but they weren't following through. Don't be afraid to hold your group members' feet to the fire. Ask them questions such as the following:

- What are you going to do this week about what God has spoken to you?
- Whom are you going to invite into a discipling relationship?

PRECONVERSION DISCIPLESHIP

Discipleship is not just for those who have confessed Jesus as King. It starts before conversion—as soon as we start showing Jesus to others.

We see several examples of Jesus building into people before they crossed any line of faith. He calls Levi out from a tax collector's booth and Zacchaeus down from a tree, just to name two. When we remove the false dichotomy of "evangelism now, discipleship later," we see many more people who need to be shaped in the way of Jesus.

Through experience I now feel comfortable forming discipling groups with a mix of people who have crossed the line of faith and people who haven't. After all, if discipleship is learning Jesus, seeking to obey him, and reproducing him in others, who doesn't need to grow in these areas? I believe that a friend of mine crossed the line of faith in my living room during a late-night discipleship group.

Some Christians who have been sitting in pews for a while have never been told there is a reproducing aspect to discipleship. I believe that with simple discipleship training we can see much fruit from pre-believers, new believers, and long-time believers.

WHERE THE RUBBER MEETS THE ROAD

Applying the six principles for a multiplying church will change things. Once you have guardrails in place, you can be more effective in using your time to multiply disciples as Jesus commissioned us to do. You will also notice hungry people who want to be discipled and who weren't on your radar before. This will inevitably change the makeup of your discipleship groups, small groups, and gospel communities. The group might not look and feel normal to you and might even make you feel uncomfortable, but the opportunities these groups present to expose people to Jesus and his church can be beautiful.

Most Christians have accidentally grouped people into

friends who know Jesus and friends who don't. Nearly every Christ follower I talk to has deep fears about creating spaces where we bring these two groups together to enjoy life and learn about Jesus. I refer to this merging as "collective overlap" and talk about this at length in my book *Staying Is the New Going*. Following the way of Jesus will lead you to uncomfortable yet beautiful situations. Just a reminder: Seek out the hungry, not the impressive. It won't be what you dreamed about, but it could be so much better.

You will need to take some risks and model vulnerability if you want to see those around you embody the holistic principle. I was in a group with a guy wrestling through whether he should move across the country to co-parent with the mother of his child or stay put. People have sought advice on family messes, business deals gone wrong, and attractions to another person other than their spouse. These are not easy, black-and-white decisions, but people need a safe Christian community to help them wrestle through how God wants them to respond to questions and challenges.

We all need people to help us walk through our messes. The community of people around us might get messier as we commit ourselves to being holistic, but over time we should begin to spend time with those Jesus would spend his time with. Remember, discipleship processes are usually not mind-blowing, but they should be consistently transformative.

In order to invest in those who might not be accepted into seminaries or chosen for the elder board, we must be willing to see people as Jesus did. Discipling with multiplication in mind will force us to give up traces of "American dream" Christianity. While Julie and I love our physical neighbors and the friends who orbit around our lives, there are moments where we would love to spend more time with mature Christians and families who look more like ours. If we only enter discipling relationships with those we are comfortable around, we have found companionship, not discipleship.

NO SILVER BULLET

Matt studied ministry at an evangelical Christian university. Terms like *evangelism*, *discipleship*, and *spiritual formation* were thrown around all the time in classes and ministries he was involved in. He even took classes entirely devoted to these concepts. Everyone was telling him that evangelism and discipleship were crucial elements of ministry. But Matt would try to reconcile what he was learning in class with what Jesus did, and it just didn't line up. In his process of searching, Matt told me, "Surely we should be able to emulate Jesus' discipleship model in our context today."

Matt is not alone. Many people, maybe you included, are trying to reconcile what they are learning in classrooms, discipleship groups, Bible studies, and sermons with how Jesus discipled others. We must be constantly spying for ways to apply what we are learning to real, everyday, gritty moments of life.

My prayer is that these six principles can form a framework that builds a bridge over what used to be a great chasm. At the end of his apprenticeship, Matt said, "There is no such thing as a perfect discipleship process, but I can say that I have yet to see principles describe the process that Jesus lived by so accurately as these six." As we look over the ministry of Jesus, I hope we look beyond Jesus' *command* to make disciples and step into his *process* of making them. Everywhere I turn, people seem to be looking for guardrails to guide them down the risks of living in the way of Jesus.

THE FRUIT REVEALS THE ROOT

We have two large apple trees in our backyard. They produce loads of apples in the fall that we churn into cider. For two years we had very few apples on the trees, and the ones that appeared were only the size of grapes. It was a bummer, to say the least. Those two years also happened to be two of the driest summers in recent history, and the roots simply had no water. Last year we had the wettest summer I can remember. While I was tired of gray skies and leaks in the basement, the branches on our apple trees were heavy with apples, and the cider jars were full. The vitality of the roots and the production of the fruit are always interconnected.

Luke 6 has much to say about this connection.

> For no good tree bears bad fruit, nor again does a
> bad tree bear good fruit, for each tree is known by
> its own fruit. For figs are not gathered from thorn-
> bushes, nor are grapes picked from a bramble bush.
> The good person out of the good treasure of his
> heart produces good, and the evil person out of his
> evil treasure produces evil, for out of the abundance
> of the heart his mouth speaks.
>
> LUKE 6:43-45

149

Disciples should be bearing fruit. It's not about production for God; it's about obedience. This "good treasure of our hearts" is our relationship with God, and the fruit is our obedience to Jesus' commands. We must not forget: *He* is the Vine, and *we* are the branches. Let's not get carried away with a desire to multiply for Jesus before we have first focused on abiding in Jesus. Love God, and he will give you the strength to love others.

What is the fruit of your life? This is always a humbling question. The answer is found in relationships. What have you cultivated in your relationship with God? What have you cultivated in your marriage? What have you cultivated in your kids? What have you cultivated in your friendships? What have you cultivated in those who wanted to learn from you? What disciples have you made? These are the questions that will define our lives. They are guardrails that keep us from stalling out or veering off course.

DISCUSSION QUESTIONS

Would others describe you as one who "has been with Jesus"? Why or why not?

On a scale of one to ten, how burdensome have your discipleship processes been?

On a scale of one to ten, how fruitful have your discipling relationships been?

What is the fruit of your discipling relationships?

12

ROADBLOCKS AND MISSING INGREDIENTS

The best measure of a spiritual life is not its ecstasies, but its obedience.
OSWALD CHAMBERS

Unsure of our direction, we double our speed.
UNKNOWN

He didn't say "you might *be my witnesses," or "you* could *be my witnesses," or even "you* should *be my witnesses." He said "you* will *be my witnesses."*
CHARLES SWINDOLL

I TOOK THE PLUNGE several years ago. I knew it was time to switch from a PC to a Mac. I had no idea a computer could be so fun to use, but I also had no idea it would take so long to adjust to. I was using similar programs, but I couldn't quite figure out the differences. For a few months I would get stuck doing simple tasks such as checking my e-mail or composing a document. I questioned whether the change was worth it several times. I wasn't making a simple switch; I was learning a whole new operating system.

If you are taking the risk to focus primarily on making disciples, you will need to make some significant shifts. If you begin to apply and live by the six principles outlined in this book, you might feel as if you are learning a new operating system. Expectations, metrics, priorities, and time management are just a few of the changes you will have to deal with. But you will find yourself with guardrails for the journey. Hang in there! It will take some recalibration and a little bit of patience, but it's worth it.

Over countless hours of conversation, I have heard many leaders express some of the following roadblocks to sustainable, multiplying ministry. These challenges will continue to surface in your ministry and will, at times, oppose these six principles. I hear these common threads from large, established churches and from small church plants across the country, and I have to resist them in my own life. I thought it valuable to share these challenges as a sort of fair warning.

The tyranny of the urgent. We will continue to be tempted to fill positions instead of making disciples. If we are honest, our first impulse is to recruit leaders instead of developing them. Many churches grow very quickly as they reach the unchurched or get transfer growth from other churches. The planter or pastor usually looks for qualified and already-equipped leaders to fill key leadership roles in the church. I often observe a church launch and become consumed with busyness that leads to a singular focus on the business of "doing church." Many of those churches never actually get around to making disciples. This tension will always be a temptation. We simply cannot afford to choose building our churches over making disciples. We must follow the progression of making disciples, developing leaders, and leading churches—in that order.

The deep-seated fear. We will be challenged with the fear

of working ourselves out of influence. We all have some fear of training others who will surpass us. One day we might even work ourselves out of a job or a volunteer ministry role. We must be selfless enough to hope those we are leading or apprenticing will rise to greater competency and influence than us. When an apprentice surpasses you, that's a great sign! We must be constantly be equipping and raising others up. In Ephesians 4 Paul reminds us that leaders are to "equip the saints for the work of ministry, for building up the body of Christ." Don't wait to develop leaders until you are looking to move out of your current role. Do it now.

Developing its *instead of* whos. We will struggle to stay people-centric rather than task-centric. We often see people for what they can accomplish. The first impulse of any leader is to pick fruit before examining the root. We must instead disciple the people God brings to us with willingness to send them where God wants them to go when he wants them to go. We will always be looking for people to delegate tasks to, but the true task of ministry is developing people. I am grateful that my leaders over the years have recognized my weaknesses and have helped shape me in many areas of my life, not just in formal ministry.

Spinning our wheels. We will be tempted toward addition instead of multiplication. Almost every spiritual leader I know was trained in good addition. This works for a while, but leaders will hit a crisis point when God gives them more influence than their schedule can handle. This is the crisis moment we examined in Acts 6. In these moments leaders must relearn discipleship through the broader lens of multiplication. I had always been taught that one-on-one discipleship is the gold standard, but suddenly I was convinced that discipling small pods of people can yield more fruit over time. I sensed God asking me, "Are you willing to change your methods so you can make more disciples?" I believe it's much more sustainable to train others in the operating system of multiplication from the start rather than having to learn it in a moment of crisis.

Fatherless parents. Most leaders in the church today have never been discipled. This presents a problem when we are sending people out to go make disciples. How can leaders become spiritual fathers and mothers if they have never been fathered or mothered themselves? Parenting is a hard thing to figure out on the fly. We must take the time to teach our people what discipleship looks, feels, and smells like as they are passing it along to others. We equip others for ministry, but I believe we also shepherd them as they walk through life.

Paralyzed with fear. We will find ourselves having to push past our own fears. We all have unique fears that paralyze us and prevent us from making disciples. Before my hinge point from addition to multiplication, I was battling fears that held me back from making disciples. These were my fears about applying the framework of movement discipleship.

- There will be no relational glue if I disciple in groups instead of one on one.
- The group setting will communicate a lack of value to each person.
- I will have to learn this discipleship process on the fly.

Ultimately, I realized that my fears were limiting my discipling capacity. I realized I was in danger of connecting these guys to me without connecting them to Jesus and to others. I have no desire to accidentally create a me-centric ministry that limits fruitfulness. You will have to identify and deal with your own fears of Kingdom multiplication. Fear can block our faith, and we must put our complete faith in God if we are ever going to experience a movement.

MISSING INGREDIENTS

I was never the straight-A valedictorian student, so whenever I took a test, I expected to miss a few questions. I learned to take great joy in getting a B. You can get a few things wrong and still pass in good form.

In baking, on the other hand, if you miss only one ingredient, you're in trouble. We've all taken a bite of a cookie where one ingredient was missing. The whole thing was off. How can a cookie be so bad when it's only missing one thing?

Discipleship is less like test taking and more like baking. We will certainly make mistakes when discipling others, but when one of these movement principles is absent, the whole discipleship process is thrown off. Use the following list to take the temperature of your discipleship processes.

Missing simplicity. People will try a complex discipleship method because they saw it work for someone else. Others struggle to make it work again, and it won't multiply long-term. This also leads to putting the leaders who discipled them on a pedestal instead of reproducing the process in others.

Missing holism. Shortsighted discipleship might work for a while, but it will head toward behavior modification. Major gaps and sin will go unaddressed because crucial areas are not "spiritual territory." Some good behavior is generated, but they never see the fullness of spiritual maturity.

Missing adaptability. A discipleship method is effective in one setting, so it is exported to another setting with very few results. It is seen as the "silver bullet" in one place while others will be frustrated because it simply isn't working in their context.

Missing regularity. Without disciplined commitment, discipleship produces spiritual flashes that fade quickly. People with shallow roots are left looking for the next spiritual high. Those you have discipled won't know how to "feed themselves" from Scripture and with a life of prayer.

Missing reproducibility. Learners fail to become instructors because they don't see themselves as "discipleship experts." They remember a time when a wise mentor led them, but they cannot figure out how to pass the process on to others. Instead of searching for Jesus, they search for another mentor.

Missing positivity. Discipleship with a negative focus will be attractive to behaviorists, and they will even think it's working. But a group that emphasizes a negative view of discipleship won't last and will die a spiritual death even before the physical death of disbanding. There are whole churches that are experiencing this and have been spiritually comatose for years.

A simple discipleship plan with a holistic emphasis that is well adapted to the particular needs of those being discipled, that has regular touch points and emphasis on consistent spiritual practices, and in which those who train others in discipleship are also reproducing themselves as disciplers, will still fall short if the focus of its discipleship is not positive. The same goes for each of these principles: To achieve most of them but to neglect one of them will inhibit your church's effectiveness in pursuing the great commission. We must be driven by a vision for being Christ's ambassadors in the world.

Recently I explored a beautiful old church building near Pittsburgh that once housed a thriving faith community. When the steel industry collapsed, so did much of this town. As I opened the large creaking door to the church, it looked as if the building had been bombed. The floor of the worship center was falling through, pews and Bibles had fallen into the fellowship hall below, and light was peeking through the ceiling from open skies above. I was grieved for the story of this church. As I closed the door, the old marquee board still read, "Triumph the Church and the Kingdom of God."

Let's not be fooled: However bleak things may seem, God is still on his throne. The effectiveness of our discipleship does not affect his love for us. Discipling relationships, leadership roles, and churches all have life cycles. We will launch faith experiments that appear to be epic failures. God's still got it. His reign and rule are everywhere triumphing over darkness in unlikely places. Whether this book finds you at the end of your rope or ready to charge hell with a water pistol, I pray that these principles bear fruit. No matter what you are feeling or what the state of your church is, there is hope.

God has been etching this book on my heart for many years. These six principles have been a gift to me, and I pray they are also a gift to you. Putting this into written form is a labor of love that will be worth it if even a few people begin to make disciples who make disciples. I believe God will continue to use his church to bring a tidal wave of his love to the world. God is multiplying the impact of his gospel in every corner of our culture. Technology is affording us opportunities to train disciples, leaders, and church planters all over the world. Hungry leaders are starting to realize they can start discipling others today. Churches are dreaming about reaching their communities again. Young leaders are seeing themselves as the church of today, not just the church of someday. I have prayed that the simple process of chaining myself to the desk and putting this in written form will be a gift to the church.

May this simple framework help you to multiply Jesus into individuals, groups, and churches all over who dare to remember that the gates of hell will not prevail against his church. May these principles help give you guardrails for the journey of making disciples of every nation, tribe, and tongue. May we wait and pray expectantly that the seeds of the Kingdom will find soft soil, take root, and bear fruit. We all are learners, and God never promises us success. It is only by his grace and our obedience that we will experience a movement. It is, indeed, all about faithfulness.

I leave you with this prayer.

Now to him who is able to do far more abundantly than all that we ask or think, according to the power at work within us, to him be glory in the church and in Christ Jesus throughout all generations, forever and ever. Amen.

EPHESIANS 3:20-24

DISCUSSION QUESTIONS

Which of the six principles are you most likely to avoid? Why?

What are your fears about adjusting your operating system to become disciple-centric?

Which tasks of ministry most easily distract you from the relationships of ministry? How will you fight against this?

EPILOGUE

I BELIEVE THAT THE PRINCIPLES in this book form a valuable framework. I also believe this is a living process. People will always be adding to and tweaking this material. I encourage you to make additions to and emphases within to this framework that make sense in your context.

One such insight came from a group of men in a church who were applying these principles. They added a seventh principle, "Realistic," because these men were running themselves ragged. They recognized that without making their goals realistic, their busy and already overcommitted leaders would burn out. I encourage you to lean into these principles and apply them creatively to your ministry and church.

Our God is the great movement maker. These words embody what I pray for all of God's people. Make sure to relax. These guardrails should give you a bit of comfort for the open road ahead.

Join the conversation and hear what I'm learning at AlanBriggs.net.

APPRENTICE CULTURE ASSESSMENT

At the 2014 Global Leadership Summit, Carly Fiorina, former CEO of Hewlett-Packard, said, "The highest calling of leadership is to unlock the potential of others." I couldn't agree more. The God-man came and unlocked a few people who would launch his church and turn the world over. Are you unlocking others' potential? Are you seeking out, affirming, and releasing others around you?

There are potential apprentices all around us. They don't know it, but many people are handcuffed, assuming that they aren't ready for ministry yet. I believe they are waiting for leaders like you to unlock them. Our churches need to be full of healthy apprenticeships for the young and old. Jesus has commissioned those around you to make disciples. Have you?

While I encourage all leaders to work toward apprenticing leaders, the first step should be assessing the health of your church culture. We need to ensure that the soil in our churches is ready to develop apprentices. It takes time and energy to develop this culture. Based on the health of the church, some are ready to multiply and some are getting healthy so they can multiply.

Here is a tool to assess your own church. Be honest, but if you are thinking critically, also be ready to think creatively about how your church can grow in these areas. Take a quick health check in these nine areas. Which tendencies do you lean toward?

APPRENTICES VERSUS INTERNS

- *Apprentices:* Your church family is equipping and showing value to hungry leaders. These apprentices are simultaneously investing in others and being invested in.
- *Interns:* You have hired hands serving in areas where you could not afford to pay anyone. No one is truly investing in them.

SENDING VERSUS PUNTING

- *Sending:* Your church celebrates and validates releasing leaders.
- *Punting:* Your church battles or threatens leaders who are leaving.

TITHING LEADERS VERSUS LIMPING LEADERS

- *Tithing leaders:* Other churches, regions, or nations are benefiting from the leaders you have equipped and sent.
- *Limping leaders:* People are leaving your church damaged or unsure of how to serve in the next church

they land in. They often struggle to find another church, and when they do, they are not a gift to that next church.

ACTIVE MINISTERS VERSUS PASSIVE LISTENERS

- *Active ministers:* Individuals in your church know that all believers are sent on mission, and they don't have to go into pastoral ministry to have an impact.
- *Passive listeners:* Your people believe the church staff are the only ones doing ministry, and they are waiting for the staff to tell them what to do.

FREEDOM VERSUS BUREAUCRACY

- *Apostolic freedom:* Out-of-the-box ministries are bubbling up through spiritual entrepreneurs. People don't need permission to minister in their spheres of influence.
- *Bureaucracy:* The red tape is so thick that unique ministries aren't emerging. People don't feel the freedom to dream about new areas and are afraid to serve God as he has wired them to.

INVESTMENT VERSUS IMPORTANCE

- *Investment:* Leaders are actively inviting others into a full life in Jesus.
- *Importance:* Congregants seek only to connect with the staff and those they deem "important."

HUNGRY VERSUS DISCONTENT

- *Hungry for a future:* Your church understands its unique vision and is working toward leaving a legacy through discipleship.
- *Discontent with the present:* Your people are grasping for any kind of future relevance or idolizing the past.

TOGETHER VERSUS ALONE

- *Together:* Your church leadership is bringing others along to partner in ministry and is giving them chances to lead.
- *Alone:* Your church leadership has a culture of doing ministry in isolation from others.

HOW VERSUS WHY

- *How:* Your people understand how to do ministry based on lasting principles for life and ministry.
- *What:* Your people are focused solely on what programs and events your church offers.

Every church has room for growth. One of these nine areas might stick out as a growth area you need to focus on during this season. Churches with an existing apprentice culture should look for ways to invite more apprentices in. Churches working toward an apprentice culture should set measurable goals to begin to offer apprenticeships under leaders who "get it." Local churches must be the breeding ground for apprenticing leaders of all kinds. The future of the church that Jesus planted depends on it.

ACKNOWLEDGMENTS

I DON'T FEEL QUALIFIED to write this book. This is all an overflow of what God and others have taught me. I have had the privilege of learning from many disciples who take Jesus seriously. Thank you all.

Thanks to the leaders and body of Vanguard Church for living a risky mission. Kelly, thank you for your faithfulness and your trust.

Thanks to apprentices for being obedient to God and coming to Colorado to follow Jesus.

Thanks to church planters and missional leaders taking risks for the gospel. You are heroes.

Thanks to my beautiful bride, Julie. You understand why this message matters so much.

Thanks for many iterations of the community that is Cultivate Learning Track for taking the adventure with me.

Thanks to those who shared your thoughts for the book: Bill, Austin, Zach, Dan, Ashley, David, and Matt. You all have bright futures and bright nows.

Thanks to the Frontline team and those who have supported Frontline Church Planting. You have helped make
this dream into a reality. Heart of the Springs, I am still
amazed by your generosity to kickstart us.

Thanks to those who have joined the mission of God
with us in our neighborhood and our city. We look forward
to more prayer and parties with you.

Thanks to Bill Lighty for dreaming big dreams for a
movement in our city.

Thanks to J. R. for everything you do as my little big
brother. I will never forget our first Bible study.

Thanks to Phil Collins, Faye Checowich, and Bob Lay.
I hated our hard conversations, but I needed them.

NOTES

CHAPTER 1: CHAOS IN SEARCH OF ORDER
1. See Dee Hock, *Birth of the Chaordic Age* (New York: Berrett-Koehler, 2000).
2. Steve Addison, *Movements That Change the World* (Downers Grove, IL: InterVarsity, 2011), 23.

CHAPTER 2: THE KINGDOM
1. Karl Barth, *Church Dogmatics* IV.3.2 (Edinburgh, Scotland: T & T Clark, 1994).
2. Shane Claiborne and Jonathan Wilson-Hartgrove, *Becoming the Answer to Our Prayers* (Downers Grove, IL: InterVarsity, 2008), 23.
3. Robert Webber and Rodney Clapp, *People of the Truth: The Power of the Worshiping Community in the Modern World* (Eugene, OR: Wipf and Stock, 1988), 39.

CHAPTER 3: THE GREAT COMMISSION
1. Simon Sinek, *Start with Why* (Steamboat Springs, CO: Portfolio, 2011), 29.
2. Dallas Willard, speaking at the Ecclesia National Gathering, Chevy Chase, MD, 2011.
3. Robert Webber and Rodney Clapp, *People of the Truth: The Power of the Worshiping Community in the Modern World* (Eugene, OR: Wipf and Stock, 1988), 37.
4. C. S. Lewis, *Mere Christianity* (San Francisco: HarperOne, 2015), 199.
5. Dietrich Bonhoeffer, *The Cost of Discipleship* (New York: Touchstone, 1995), 64.
6. Steve Addison, *Movements That Change the World* (Downers Grove, IL: InterVarsity, 2011), 97.

GUARDRAILS

7. Addison, *Movements That Change the World,* 29.
8. Neil Cole, *Organic Leadership* (Grand Rapids, MI: Baker, 2010), 27.
9. Eric Hoffer, quoted in Addison, *Movements That Change the World,* 103.

CHAPTER 4: THE APPRENTICE
1. Neil Cole, speaking at the Multiply Conference, Colorado Springs, Colorado, September 2014.
2. Ibid.
3. John Maxwell, *The Five Levels of Leadership: Proven Steps to Maximize Your Potential* (New York: Center Street, 2011).
4. Roland Allen, *The Spontaneous Expansion of the Church* (Portland, OR: Wipf & Stock, 1997), 20–21.
5. Alan Hirsch and Michael Frost, *The Faith of Leap* (Grand Rapids, MI: Baker, 2011), 44–45. Italics in original.

CHAPTER 5: DISCIPLESHIP MUST BE SIMPLE
1. Father Herbert Kelly, quoted in Roland Allen, *The Spontaneous Expansion of the Church* (Portland, OR: Wipf and Stock, 1997), 140.
2. Dave Ferguson and Alan Hirsch, *On the Verge* (Grand Rapids, MI: Zondervan, 2011), 287.
3. Mike Breen, *Building a Discipling Culture* (Pawleys Island, SC: 3DM Publishing, 2014), 17.

CHAPTER 6: DISCIPLESHIP MUST BE HOLISTIC
1. Alan and Debra Hirsch, *Untamed* (Grand Rapids, MI: Baker, 2010), 62–63.

CHAPTER 7: DISCIPLESHIP MUST BE ADAPTABLE
1. David Bosch, *Transforming Mission* (New York: Orbis, 2011), 2–3.
2. Steve Addison, *Movements That Change the World* (Downers Grove, IL: InterVarsity, 2011), 24.
3. Rodney Stark, *The Rise of Christianity* (San Francisco: HarperOne, 1997), 3.

CHAPTER 9: DISCIPLESHIP MUST BE REPRODUCIBLE
1. Read Ying Kai's story in the book by Steve Smith and Ying Kai, *T4T: A Discipleship Re-Revolution* (Midlothian, VA: WigTake Resources, 2011).
2. Neil Cole, *Organic Leadership* (Grand Rapids, MI: Baker, 2010), 152.
3. Michael Gerber, *The E-Myth Revisited* (New York: HarperCollins, 2004), 100.
4. You can read about the heart behind the Epic Fail conference and what God has taught J. R. through these gatherings in his book *Fail* (Downers Grove, IL: InterVarsity, 2014).

170

5. David Garrison, *Church Planting Movements* (Midlothian, VA: WigTake Resources, 2004), 292.
6. Ed Stetzer, "Five Characteristics of Transformative Small Groups," *The Exchange* (blog), *Christianity Today*, July 12, 2012, http://www.christianity today.com/edstetzer/2012/july/five-characteristics-of-transformative-small -groups.html.
7. Steve Addison, *Movements That Change the World* (Downers Grove, IL: InterVarsity, 2011), 98, 137.
8. Smith and Ying Kai, *T4T: A Discipleship Re-Revolution*, 115.

CHAPTER 10: DISCIPLESHIP MUST BE POSITIVE

1. Thanks to my brilliant brother, J. R. Briggs, for pointing me to this diagram from John Ortberg, *The Me I Want to Be* (Grand Rapids, MI: Zondervan, 2009). Used by permission.

CHAPTER 11: APPLYING MOVEMENT PRINCIPLES

1. Steve Addison, *Movements That Change the World* (Downers Grove, IL: InterVarsity, 2011), 28.

ABOUT THE AUTHOR

ALAN BRIGGS lives with his wife, Julie, and their four kids in Colorado Springs, where they are committed to dwelling well in their neighborhood. He loves those inside and outside the church, but he finds deep joy in equipping the saints for ministry (Ephesians 4:12). He is the director of Frontline Church Planting, where he networks and equips leaders to multiply disciples, leaders, and churches in Colorado and beyond. He is also the multiplying pastor at Vanguard Church. His first book, *Staying Is the New Going*, shares a vision for a call back to faithful presence in the cities and seasons in which we've been placed. He continues to pray for a major movement of God in Colorado. He loves tacos, upscale pancakes, and seriously competitive sports like bocce ball.

@AlanBriggs
AlanBriggs.net

Frontline exists to equip the saints to multiply
DISCIPLES >> LEADERS >> CHURCHES.

Every church—big and small, new and old—can multiply, and we want to help.

Frontline connects and equips leaders in the following ways:

- Monthly on-the-ground equipping for everyday missionaries, church planters, and church leaders
- Frontline Church Planting residency
- Online training and coaching
- Church multiplication consulting
- Network gatherings, roundtables, and meetups
- Our annual MULTIPLY conference in Colorado

FrontlineChurchPlanting.com

FRONTLINE
CHURCH
PLANTING

DISCIPLES LEADERS CHURCHES

CP0965

YOU HAVE NEIGHBORS. YOU'RE IN RELATIONSHIPS.
——————— YOU LIVE SOMEWHERE. ———————

WHAT IF YOU STAYED?

#stayingisthenewgoing
#stayforth

AVAILABLE AT NAVPRESS.COM OR WHEREVER BOOKS ARE SOLD.

CP1005